The Iliad Interpreted for Content Creators

How Ego, Competition, and Alliances Shape Creative Power

ANCIENT WISDOM HACKS

Third Edition

Table of Contents

Epigraph

"Sing, O goddess, the wrath of Achilles, Peleus' son."
Homer's opening plea to the Muse reminds every modern creator that before we hit "publish" we, too, call upon something larger than ourselves—insight, inspiration, community—to give our work force and fluency.

Preface

I grew up skimming Homer for school, neat lines tucked between soccer practice and late-night TV. Years later, running a content agency and drowning in click-driven advice, I reopened *The Iliad*—and realized I was holding a blueprint. Heroes fighting for attention, bards battling obscurity, audiences chanting back lines they knew by heart. The poem wasn't ancient; it was a live feed. This book distills that discovery: marketing wisdom hidden in bronze and blood, sharpened so today's writers, streamers and founders can wield it fast. If Homer could keep camp-fires rapt for ten years straight, we can hold a timeline for ten seconds—once we learn his moves.

Acknowledgments

Deep thanks to the classicists who keep the epic's pulse audible: Caroline Alexander for her lucid translation notes, Emily Wilson for reminding me Homer still sings, and the late Richmond Lattimore whose cadence first hooked me. Gratitude to my content mentors—Josh Spector, Amanda Natividad, Jay Clouse—who prove that generosity scales. To the beta readers who flagged jargon, pushed for sharper edges, and never let me hide behind mythic fog: you made this book a tighter spear. Finally, to every subscriber who hit "reply" instead of scrolling on—your feedback is my camp-fire chorus.

Introduction: Why a Bronze-Age Epic Still Sells Today

Homer's poem is the oldest viral story in Western literature. Long before printing presses or push notifications, *The Iliad* spread by word of mouth, leaping coastlines on the lips of traveling bards. Audiences knew the plot, yet packed in each night to hear it "sung again"—proof that freshness comes not only from novelty but from delivery, relevance, and emotional stakes.

Oral tradition was the original creator economy. Performers exchanged narrative for food, shelter, and fame; patrons gained status by hosting the hottest voice in the Aegean. Every retelling carried tweaks—local shout-outs, inside jokes—much like today's creators remix trends to fit their niche while keeping the core hook intact.

Our goal is simple: turn epic motifs into repeatable creative systems. Achilles' singular focus becomes niche mastery. The duels on the plain become one-to-one audience engagement. Even the gods meddling from Olympus mirror algorithm shifts that bless or punish posts. By translating these patterns into frameworks and action steps, you'll wield ancient tactics with modern speed.

Road-map of the chapters
 Part I seeds mindset: invoke your Muse, own your Achilles-level edge, curb hubris before it burns your brand.
 Part II forges armor: world-build like Hephaestus, master metaphor, turn lists into momentum.
 Part III covers battle tactics: spar in public, rally the crowd, slip collaborators inside Trojan-horse content.
 Part IV deals with the gods—platform biases, format balance, smart ad spend.
 Part V teaches siege endurance: build a Myrmidon inner circle, defuse burnout, and close arcs with funeral-game flourish.

By the final page, you'll have a strategic kit tested not in boardrooms but on a thousand-year field of war stories. The Muse is listening. Time to sing.

Chapter 1 – Summon the Muse: Finding Your Core Narrative

"Sing, O goddess, the wrath of Achilles, Peleus' son,
 that brought infinite sorrows upon the Achaeans."

Homer does not begin with a plot summary, a weather report, or an info-dump of bronze-age trivia. He begins with a plea—for voice, for force, for clarity. The very first verb is *sing*. The very first noun is *wrath*. From that pairing comes the gravitational center of the poem, the north-star theme that steers every scene to come. Before the armies march or the gods descend, the poet fixes our attention on a single hot point of tension: Achilles' rage.

Modern creators face different battlefields—feeds, inboxes, search rankings—but the principle is identical. Without an anchored theme your content drifts, your audience drifts with it, and even your own enthusiasm leaks away. Invoking the Muse is less about supernatural help than about locking on to a direction so pure that you cannot mistake the next step. The pages ahead will walk you through that lock-on process. Treat it as your first ritual: a sharpened moment in which you ask, aloud if you dare, "What am I really here to sing?"

The Lesson: From Invocation to Orientation

When Homer croons, "Sing, goddess," he is not begging for random inspiration; he is specifying topic, tone, and stakes in one breath. The phrase that follows—"the wrath of Achilles"—acts like a branding tagline hammered into the shield of the poem. Every clash, every plea to heaven, every death in the dust swings back to this magnetic phrase. Even the gods' bickering becomes a ripple off Achilles' anger.

Creators need an equivalent. Call it your *north-star theme,* your *brand marrow,* or the *wrath line*—the single sentence that concentrates your driving tension. "But wrath sounds negative," you might protest. True; not every project burns with ire. Yet behind every memorable creator sits some charged emotion: indignation at bad design, awe at the cosmos, curiosity about lost cuisines, delight in comedic absurdity, hunger to lift marginalized voices. Wrath is shorthand for that voltage. Once named, it powers the machinery of content decisions from topic selection to tonal quirks.

Action Step 1: Write Your One-Sentence "Wrath Line"

1. **Surface Your Tension.**
   Begin with raw, maybe messy statements that explain why you care. Free-write for ten minutes without aiming for polish. Ask:
   What infuriates me?
   What excites me so strongly I rant without noticing time?
   What gap in the world won't leave me alone?
   Example scribbles might read:
   "I hate how jargon walls ordinary people out of science."
   "I can't stop thinking about why creative women over forty

vanish from spotlight."
Do not self-censor; this is heat-mining.

2. **Distill to a Core Verb and Noun.**
   Homer pairs *sing* (verb) with *wrath* (noun). Try the same
   pattern. Strip your statement to an action and an object. If
   your draft says, "I want to show people that city history
   hides in plain sight," test verbs like *reveal, unearth,
   spotlight,* then nouns like *history, legends, secrets.* Mix
   until a phrase snaps into focus:
   Reveal forgotten city legends.

3. **Draft the Wrath Line.**
   Fuse verb and object with a pinch of context or audience.
   One breathable sentence, fifteen words or fewer.
   Examples:
   *"Unearth forgotten city legends so locals feel at home in
   their own streets."*
   *"Demystify money so first-gen kids can outmaneuver debt,
   not drown in it."*
   *"Reclaim pop culture for disabled fans who rarely see
   themselves onstage."*
   Tight. Punchy. Memorizable.

4. **Pressure-Test for Direction.**
   Throw future content ideas against the line. Does each
   idea either illustrate, advance, or challenge it? If not, cut or
   pivot the idea. The wrath line is not a slogan for your
   website header (though it can be); it is a compass you
   check quietly before every creative march.

5. **Say It Aloud Three Times.**
   Sound is memory's glue. Homeric bards performed, not printed. By speaking your line you hear awkward clunks, extra syllables, or emotional false notes. Tweak until it rolls off your tongue like a mantra you could, yes, sing.

Action Step 2: Develop a Personal Mythos Statement

Achilles' wrath may be the theme, but the poem also supplies his lineage, "Peleus' son," and a prophecy-infused arc, hinting at glory and doom. That layered backstory forms his *mythos.* Your content deserves the same narrative scaffolding: not just what you do, but who you are, how you arrived, and where this road could lead. Readers follow people, not RSS feeds.

a. Chart the Three Roots

1. **Origin:**
   The catalyzing moment that set you on this path. It might be the night you bombed a stand-up set and vowed to master storytelling, or the afternoon you watched a small business shutter because of one legal loophole. Capture it in vivid, sensory detail.

2. **Transformation:**
   Show the audience the forge where your current skills were hammered. Courses, apprenticeships, late-night experiments—all highlight the credibility of lived labor over

borrowed wisdom.

3. **Horizon:**
   Achilles knows he is fated for early death if he chases glory. That knowledge charges his every decision. Your mythos should glance forward too: the change you seek in the industry, the community you dream to build, the legacy you hope your content leaves.

b. Shape the Narrative Arc

Compress the three roots into a Roman-road paragraph: clear, direct, propulsive. Example:

"I grew up translating my immigrant mother's medical bills, watching simple words gatekeep life-and-death decisions. After a decade training as a technical writer, I realized clarity saves more than time—it saves dignity. Now I decode bureaucratic language so every patient understands their own body's paperwork, and I won't stop until hospitals treat transparency as standard care."

c. Infuse Voice

Avoid corporate buzz. Slip in rhythm, metaphors, even a fragment of humor if that suits your brand. The mythos statement is a story told fireside, not a résumé bullet.

d. Iterate with Context

Different platforms require different cuts. A Twitter bio version might shrink to: "Former kid translator. Now decoding medical jargon for patients everywhere." The backbone stays; the outfit changes.

Action Step 3: The Litmus Test

Homer's lines stuck because they were repeated by thousands of jaws across centuries. You need no such epoch, but you do need the *memorability* check. Choose an idolized follower—someone you respect in your niche, whose opinion carries weight. Imagine they encounter your line once in a podcast intro and then repeat it at dinner. Could they get the gist right?

How to Test:

1. **Find a Trusted Peer.**
   Send them your wrath line and mythos statement. Ask them to recite it the next day unprompted.

2. **Measure Fidelity.**
   If they recall only foggy fragments, your line lacks hook or brevity. Trim adjectives, sharpen verbs, swap generic nouns for concrete ones.

3. **Check Emotional Impact.**
   Ask them what feeling the line gave. Indifference is a warning flare. Adjust tone until an emotion—excitement, outrage, hope—sparks on first hearing.

A phrase from *The Iliad* often quoted is "short life and long fame." Brevity plus resonance. Your line must achieve the same.

Deep Dive: Anatomy of Homer's Opening

"Sing, goddess, the wrath of Achilles, Peleus' son, that brought countless ills upon the Achaeans." The sentence carries five structural moves worth copying.

1. **Invocation:** *Sing, goddess*—a direct call to power beyond the self. Even atheists can channel this by addressing *reason, community,* or *imagination.* Lead with an imperative. It forces alertness.

2. **Theme Declaration:** *the wrath of Achilles*—no hedging. Name the core in plain language.

3. **Character Marker:** *Peleus' son*—contextual grounding. Your theme should attach to a who, even if that who is you or your avatar audience.

4. **Consequence Signal:** *that brought countless ills*—hint at stakes. Why should the audience lean in?

5. **Collective Impact:** *upon the Achaeans*—scope. Who will feel the shockwaves?

Craft your own invocation sentence by sentence, then condense into the wrath line. Example draft:

"Guide me, insight, to expose the silent costs of cheap fashion, that rob beauty from maker and planet alike."

Now compress:

"Expose the silent costs of cheap fashion."

Examples in the Wild

Case 1: Tech Educator
 Original rambly vision: "I like making complex computer stuff easy."
 Wrath line after refinement: "Demystify AI so non-coders can bend it to human dreams, not corporate profit."
 Memorability proof: Students quoted it back on day two of a workshop.

Case 2: Culinary Historian
 Wrath line: "Resurrect lost flavors from forgotten diasporas."
 Personal mythos: Childhood taste of grandmother's vanished herb sparked a quest across archives and kitchens.

In both cases the line became not only branding but a filter: sponsorship offers, guest-post invites, even merch ideas had to echo the phrasing or be declined.

Ritualizing Your Invocation

Homer's bards repeated the opening lines at every performance, a neural cue that shifted both singer and listeners into mythic space. Adopt your own micro-ritual before creating:

Voice Note Invocation
Record yourself reciting the wrath line. Play it back as you open your laptop.

Call-and-Response
If streaming, start sessions by speaking the line and inviting chat to echo keywords in text form.

Muse Token
Keep a physical object—a stone, a stylus, a mini statue on your desk. Touch it while repeating the line to anchor focus.

Such gestures might feel theatrical, yet theatre is exactly how oral tradition cemented memory. Treat mindset as muscle; ritual is warm-up.

Common Pitfalls and Antidotes

1. **Vagueness**
   "Share knowledge to inspire others."
   Antidote: Insert a tangible outcome and a target audience:
   "Teach indie designers to price art without apology."

2. **Over-stuffed Statements**
   The wrath line is not a Swiss-army biography. If you cram five goals, none will stick. Store secondary aims in sub-themes or future chapters.

3. **Trend-Locked Language**
   Slang ages faster than yogurt in the sun. Choose words that survive algorithm seasons. Achilles' rage lives

millennia because *rage* is timeless, *lit AF* less so.

4. **Borrowed Passion**
   Beware adopting a cause only because it is marketable.
   Achilles' wrath succeeds because it is intrinsic, not
   brand-strategy fluff. Authentic fireoutsells synthetic sparks
   every cycle.

Integrating the Core Narrative Across Channels

Blog posts become deeper dives into sub-questions of the wrath
line.
Newsletters recap progress in the quest implied by your mythos.
Short-form video dramatizes single moments where your tension
peaks.
Podcasts invite guests who embody or challenge your theme,
turning dialogue into duel.

Align design elements too. A historian of lost cuisines might
employ archival textures and faded recipes as background motifs.
A clarity-first technical writer might keep layouts spare,
monospace headlines echoing code blocks. Visuals should hum
the same note as the wrath line's syllables.

Sustaining the North-Star Over Time

Passion ebbs; even Achilles sulks in his tent. Build maintenance habits:

Quarterly Re-Invocation
Set a date to revisit the wrath line under fresh light. Has your audience changed? Has the industry pivoted? Keep the spine but allow muscles to adapt.

Story Bank
Collect anecdotes that reinforce your mythos. When doubt creeps, skim the bank to remember why you began.

Audience Echoes
Screenshot comments where followers paraphrase your line. These echoes prove resonance and refill resolve.

When to Pivot the Line

Signs include:

- You feel bored reciting it.

- Your content ideas strain to connect.

- Audiences misinterpret your purpose despite clarity attempts.

Pivot, but publicly acknowledge the shift. Homer would announce catalogue updates; so should you. Transparency turns mutation into maturation.

Finishing Challenge

Within twenty-four hours of reading this chapter, draft your wrath line and mythos paragraph. Speak them on camera or microphone—even if you never publish the clip. Hearing yourself articulate the theme anchors it in muscle memory. Next, place the lines at the top of your workspace, whether sticky note or screensaver. For the coming week let every creative decision orbit this nucleus.

Remember the opening image of *The Iliad*: a singer under starlight, soldiers leaned forward, waiting not for news—they all knew the story—but for the unique electricity of this voice tonight. Your audience, dispersed across screens, waits the same way. Summon your Muse with clarity, and even the algorithm becomes a camp-fire breeze that carries your words farther than bronze arrows ever flew.

Chapter 2 – Know Thy Achilles: Niche Domination & Signature Strength

> "But I, I tell you this—
> there is no man of the Achaeans swift or strong enough
> to fight beside me when I unleash my power."

Achilles steps onto the plain of Troy not as one more bronze-helmed warrior but as the living edge of Greek ambition. His name alone tilts morale, war calculus, even the moods of the gods. The poet hammers that fact again and again—"swift-footed Achilles, best of the Achaeans"—because in a clamor of nearly identical helmets, one staggering superiority becomes a moat no enemy can ford. Your creator journey demands the same moat. It requires a skill so honed that when you unveil it, rivals reconsider their campaigns and audiences lean closer, sure they will see something impossible.

LESSON: Achilles' Incomparable Skill Equals a Brand Moat

Achilles does not dabble. He does not juggle repertoire the way Odysseus shifts disguises. His spear work is so focused it borders on obsession. That focus produces two effects any creator should crave. First, his uniqueness simplifies choice for allies: if the Greeks need an unstoppable strike, they know the call. Second, it distorts competition. Hector is mighty, yet every clash narrative hinges on one question—will Achilles fight today? The field and its thousand swords shrink into a single axis of suspense around a single capability.

Translating this to modern work: a signature strength locks attention, resources, and algorithmic favor in your direction. Let rivals diversify; you double down. Let them flaunt sprawling offers; you become legendary for one definitive move. People remember the best at one thing faster than the competent at ten.

STRATEGY: Map Strengths vs Market Gaps to Claim an Achilles-Heel You Control

The phrase "Achilles heel" usually signals weakness, yet in our tactical repurposing it denotes a pressure point in the market no one else exploits—one you strike at will because it lies under your mastery. You discover it where three zones overlap:

1. **Innate or trained strength** – the craft you perform with minimal friction and maximal joy.

2. **Audience hunger** – a pain or desire underserved by current options.

3. **Competitive gap** – a space others overlook, resist, or simply cannot fill due to their own brand physics.

Mapping this Venn demands data, honesty, and strategic ruthlessness—qualities Achilles exudes when he assesses battlefield stakes. He does not sprint at every skirmish. He waits, calculates, ensures the next appearance carves immortal echo. Likewise you must resist scattering output across fleeting trends and instead pour kinetic energy into your singular strike.

Step One: Internal Landscape—Skill Inventory

Begin with brutal clarity. Achilles boasts, "No man can match me," because evidence backs him. You must collect your evidence. Catalogue every competence. Rate each on three metrics: mastery, energy, and proof. Mastery asks how reliably you produce elite results. Energy asks how alive you feel mid-execution. Proof asks for visible impact—audience reaction, revenue, transformation. Many creators assume a skill stands tall because it feels good; record whether others confirm. Achilles' kill count is public record in the dust. Seek your own dust-particle numbers: testimonials, completion rates, click-through lifts, speaking invites.

As you mark scores, watch for spikes where all three metrics converge. A 9 in mastery but a 3 in energy foretells burnout. A 9 in energy but a 4 in proof might be hobby, not brand weapon. The goal is the spot where excellence, enthusiasm, and evidence fuse. Label these candidate signature strengths.

Step Two: External Landscape—Competitor "Trojan Wall" Audit

Homer's Greeks spend years probing Troy's defenses before the final ruse. You will spend a fraction of that time but equal cunning examining rivals. The Trojan walls you face are the entrenched offerings, tone, and rhythms of top creators in your field. Audit at least ten voices: five giants everyone references, three rising players, two wildcards who break rules. For each, note:

- Core promise: what line sits at the heart of their pitch?

- Delivery edge: which formats or atmospheres they own?

- Weak signal: cracks where they falter—slow replies, dated visuals, missing subtopics.

As you map this, patterns emerge—themes saturated, gaps yawning. Perhaps every productivity guru pumps out bullet-list hacks but few show failures in real-time. Maybe food channels flood thirty-second recipes yet ignore science-backed nutrition nuance. List these vacancies beside your candidate strengths. When correlation clicks—your gift matches their neglect—you have located the Achilles heel.

Step Three: Opportunity Matrix—Choose a Strike Zone

Overlay your internal spikes atop external vacancies. Rate potential strike zones by three filters:

1. **Barrier to entry for others** – how hard is it for a rival to copy or catch up? Achilles' speed is genetics soldered to training: near-impossible to duplicate.

2. **Scalability** – can this strength translate across platforms or products without diluting its power?

3. **Narrative potency** – does this strength resonate with mythic clarity? Will audiences grasp it in one sentence?

Whichever zone scores highest becomes your signature battleground. Commit publicly. Stake your banner so allies and foes both adjust expectations.

EXERCISES

1. Detailed Skill Inventory

Set aside three uninterrupted hours. Split a page into two columns: *Raw Skills* and *Proof Points.* Under Raw Skills, brain-dump everything from editing long-form essays to weaving memes. Under Proof Points, attach hard evidence—metrics, screenshots, awards, public praise. Circle every entry supported by triple proof: numbers, reputation, influence. These circles are preliminary Achilles indicators.

Now interrogate emotional resonance. Next to every circled skill, scribble a one-to-ten energy score—ten when you lose sense of time performing it, one when you want a nap. Discard anything below seven. Achilles fights because battle sings in his blood; your signature skill should feel like oxygen, not obligation.

2. Competitor "Trojan Wall" Audit

Take a fresh notebook or digital board. Write each competitor's name at the top of a sheet. Under headings *Promise, Delivery Edge, Weak Signal,* fill details gleaned from binge-watching their public work. Hunt for subtleties: Are comment sections filled with unanswered questions? Do their visuals plateau while copy sparkles? Put stars next to weak signals aligning with your high-energy skill.

Next, sketch a miniature Trojan horse beside each starred opening. Inside the horse, list content formats you could roll through that gap—threads, tutorials, live reverse-engineering sessions, challenge cohorts. This visual anchor reminds you that domination rarely happens head-on; it slips past fortifications through craft and surprise.

3. 30-Day Sprint to Sharpen One Unfair Advantage

Select the single strength that best meets the Opportunity Matrix. Commit to a month of concentrated hypertrophy. Achilles trains with divine armor and constant sparring; you will do likewise. The sprint includes four weekly cycles:

Week 1: Baseline and Micro-Skills

- Record a live demonstration of the skill at current level.

- Break the skill into component moves. If it's storytelling, moves might be hook, tension escalation, sensory layering.

- Design micro-drills: one exercise per component daily, twenty minutes each.

Week 2: Volume Over Comfort

- Publish or share the skill publicly every day, regardless of polish, to build tolerance and real-world data.

- Solicit focused critique on one metric (clarity, pacing, polish) from trusted critics.

- Log improvements in a sprint journal.

Week 3: Edge Experimentation

- Introduce a constraint that forces innovation—time cap, unfamiliar subject, blindfold sketch if visual.

- Monitor which experiments spark disproportionate engagement or create flow jolts.

- Save the top three breakout variations for refinement.

Week 4: Signature Codification

- Choose one breakout variation and craft a repeatable framework.

- Produce a masterclass-style piece—thread, video, guide—showing process start to finish.

- Pin this artifact across channels as the definitive proof of your ascendant moat.

The sprint ends with a reflection letter: What shifted in metrics, audience perception, self-efficacy? Achilles' rampage after Patroclus' death is no accident; it is the climax of years of combat layering on raw rage. Document your layers so future spurts compound, not stall.

Embedding Signature Strength into Brand DNA

A moat unadvertised is merely a puddle. Once sharpened, the strength must saturate every brand molecule:

- **Handles & Headlines** – weave the strength verb into your username, tagline, podcast intro.

- **Visual Motif** – Achilles' shield gleams distinct; design color or iconography that signals your weapon at a glance.

- **Content Cadence** – maintain at least one weekly piece where the skill sits center-stage so new audiences instantly witness your edge.

- **Product Ladder** – free taste (newsletter tip), mid-tier workshop, premium immersion—all orbit the signature skill.

Remember Homer's formula: each appearance of Achilles re-proves his supremacy. Consistency cements legend.

Warning: Hubris vs Moat

Achilles' edge tempts arrogance. He withholds combat to punish Agamemnon, and the Greek campaign nearly implodes. A creator can likewise suffocate growth by believing their strength excuses discipline or adaptation. Safeguard with three humility anchors:

1. **Mentor Check-ins** – monthly calls with peers who can critique blind spots.

2. **Edge Relevance Scan** – quarterly review of market chatter to ensure your strength still solves urgent pain.

3. **Learner's Challenge** – annually, study a beginner skill unrelated to your field to remember the taste of struggle.

The moat protects you from imitation, not from stagnation.

Battle Stories: Modern Achilles Illustrations

The Animator Who Frames Feelings
A freelance animator realized her sketches captured micro-expressions most colleagues glossed over. She studied facial anatomy nights, posted daily ten-second emotion loops online. Within a year Pixar recruiters DM'd her; they could mimic software effects but not her nerve-deep empathy for muscle ticks. Her moat: emotional accuracy.

The Lawyer Who Translates Law for Gamers
He loved esports contracts and despised the gibberish aimed at teenage streamers. He wrote "lawsplainer" Twitter threads, each topping with a meme from the latest game. Competitors offered dry PDF guides; he became the go-to gladiator for digital athlete rights. His moat: legal clarity blended with subculture literacy.

In both tales, signature strength pairs an elite skill with a vacuum. Results echo Achilles: audiences take sides, allies rally, and opposition rethinks strategy rather than engage head-to-head.

Closing Invocation

> "And the son of Peleus stood among the ships,
>   his heart still raging like a caged lion deprived of its
>   kill."

Channel that contained ferocity. Stand among the fleets of bland content and feel the muscle of your chosen weapon coil. The roar you launch across the plain will not always be battle; sometimes it is an elegant tutorial, a searing essay, a code snippet so brilliant it brushes on poetry. Whatever form your strike takes, let it carry the unmistakable signature of the one force only you can unleash. When the time comes—perhaps tomorrow at dawn, perhaps in the hush after a conference keynote—step forward and let every spectator sense what Hector felt: this field shifts now because you have entered it.

The moat is dug. The spear is balanced. Know thy Achilles, then go make the earth quake.

Chapter 3 – Honor & Hubris: Balancing Confidence with Community

"Sing, goddess, of the ruinous wrath of Achilles,
whose pride sent many brave souls to Hades
and left their bodies the feast of dogs and birds."

The *Iliad* teaches that greatness can turn on itself like a swung blade. Achilles is the most lethal human in the poem, yet his wounded ego—"ruinous wrath"—almost hands Troy a victory. He abandons his comrades because Agamemnon offends his honor, and the armies of Greece pay in blood.

Creators face a quieter stage but the same tension. The attention you earn can inflate certainty until you stop listening and start dictating. Followers drift, algorithms chill, and one sloppy misstep becomes a screen-shot tribunal. The antidote is proactive humility: a system of checks, rituals, and rescue ropes that keep confidence sharp but sheathed.

LESSON: Pride Nearly Sank the Greeks

Achilles' pride flares the moment Agamemnon seizes Briseïs, "the girl I won with my spear." Achilles explodes: "You people fight to keep what is yours; I fight for my honor." Then he sits out. Morale collapses, troops die, and even the gods grouse about Greek folly.

Only when Patroclus falls does Achilles re-enter the war, discovering too late that defense of ego cost the lives he meant to protect.

Our online equivalents surface as:

- ignoring early criticism because downloads look healthy,

- lashing out at a petty comment with screenshot dunking,

- ghosting collaborators after a contract glitch.

Each gesture earns short-term self-soothing, long-term fracture. Honor—your sense of value—must stand; hubris—your certainty you are above error—must kneel. The following tactics train that stance.

TACTIC 1 – Build "Troop Feedback Loops"

In bronze-age trenches a runner shouts fresh intel from the front; commanders adjust spear lines. Your digital trenches need equal agility. The Troop Feedback Loop is a micro-feedback circuit you trigger on a rhythm so tight problems have no time to metastasize.

a. Establish Signal Outposts
Choose two lightweight channels where allies can speak fast and freely. Examples: a private Discord channel labeled *battle-chatter* or a Google Form with three fields. Keep the form evergreen at the

same URL so people memorize the path. Announce publicly you monitor these outposts weekly.

b. Set the Question Cadence
Once a week drop a single focused question:

- "What topic did I forget this week that you wished I covered?"

- "Which explanation felt muddy?"
  Never more than one question. Simplicity breeds reply. Post the question at a predictable hour—Friday noon maybe—so the loop becomes ritual.

c. Train the Runners
Recruit two to five super-fans or team members as "runners" who scan replies, flag duplicates, and highlight urgent signals. Achilles trusts Patroclus to relay truth; you need a Patroclus crew. Reward them with early looks at drafts or cameo shout-outs to honor their labor.

d. Debrief in Public
Every Monday publish a quick "Intel Received" note. Summarize top themes, note one immediate fix, and one item queued for research. This shows the army you listened and keeps you accountable.

e. Evaluate Quarterly
Review 12 weeks of loops. Map complaints that recur more than twice. These patterns reveal where hubris lurks—places you assumed mastery. Draft a learning sprint or hiring plan to patch.

Troop Feedback Loops keep ego porous: praise flows in, but so does critique, cushioning the shock of larger storms.

TACTIC 2 – Rituals for Humility

Soldiers pour wine to the gods before eating; rituals frame survival. You need recurring acts that shrink self-importance and inflate community acknowledgment.

Weekly Gratitude Thread

Every Sunday launch a thread or newsletter footer titled "Torch-Passing." List three contributors to your growth that week—could be a reviewer who caught a typo, a commenter who shared a personal story, or a rival who wrote something so good it pushed you to revise. Tag them or link their work. The rules:

1. **Specificity over flattery**
   "@Nia flagged that my audio peaked at 2:13—saved the episode."

2. **Non-transactional**
   Do not pair thanks with a sales ask. This is gift, not lead magnet.

3. **Consistent timing**
   Predictability breeds participation; followers begin nominating peers in response, compounding communal lift.

After twelve weeks, compile highlights into a "Roll of Honor" blog post. The effect mirrors Homeric catalogues: names etched for all time, motivating continued excellence.

Highlight a Follower

Once a month hand over a slice of your platform: a guest newsletter slot, a five-minute live segment, an Instagram takeover. Requirements:

- The follower chooses topic, angle, and call-to-action (within ethical bounds).

- You introduce them with context: how you crossed paths, what you admire.

- You stay in comments to cheerlead.

This inversion demonstrates that audience voices matter as much as yours. It also inoculates against the Achilles sulk; when you watch someone step into your light and the sky does not fall, you realize spotlight is abundant.

Personal Debrief Ceremony

Set midmonth calendar block named "Hubris Check." Agenda:

1. **Replay Tape**
   Watch or read one piece of content from six months ago. Mark sloppy segments.

2. **Note Audience Shifts**
   Compare metrics or comments. Where did engagement
   dip? Is it style drift or market change?

3. **Offer Tribute**
   Email or DM a creator you learned from recently—no ask,
   pure salute.

Document reflections in a private journal. Over quarters, patterns
of mistake emerge; you build humility muscle memory.

TACTIC 3 – Crisis Plan for Inevitable Missteps

Even with loops and rituals, arrows of error fly. A client might
accuse you of plagiarism; you might tweet an insensitive joke;
your paid course could launch with a broken checkout. Achilles'
crisis—Patroclus' death—forces him to reconcile pride with
collective survival. Better design your response now than
improvise under fire.

Stage One: Rapid Acknowledgment (0–2 hours)

- **Locate Facts** – consult logs, screenshots, or team
  accounts.

- **Issue Holding Statement** – one short public post: "I've
  learned X may have occurred. I'm investigating and will

update in 24 hours."

- **Close Mouth Elsewhere** – do not argue in comments. Save data.

Stage Two: Clarity & Apology (2–24 hours)

Craft an apology that follows the tripartite Homeric plea style: admit offense, name harm, promise action.

> "Friends, hear me. In my haste I published research uncredited. This disrespected the original author and betrayed your trust. I am removing the post, compensating the scholar, and implementing a new citation review before anything goes live."

Attach hard fixes—refund links, corrected docs, new policy bullets.

Stage Three: Community Revision Council (Day 2–Day 14)

Invite a small, diverse subset of your audience to review the fix. Maybe they beta-test the revised course or vet language. Publish their feedback alongside final patch. This signals you value external perspectives.

Stage Four: Legacy Placement (Month 2)

Record a behind-the-scenes episode dissecting the misstep, explaining safeguards added. Pin it. Achilles learns too late, but poets narrate it so future warriors absorb the moral. Own your parable.

PUTTING THE SYSTEM TOGETHER

Imagine a timeline. Week after week you run Troop Feedback Loops and Gratitude Threads. Months roll; you highlight followers, adjust content, stay open. Suddenly a storm hits—your sponsorship with a soft-drink company angers eco-minded fans. Because the loops exist, you detect outrage in hours. Gratitude ritual has cultivated goodwill; people assume good faith and wait to hear you. Crisis plan deploys: holding statement, refund options, pivot to a local reusable-bottle firm. Two weeks later, a Revision Council publishes a verdict: "They listened, changed supplier, and donated proceeds to marine cleanup." Followers feel part of victory. Confidence returns, tempered.

Without the loops, hubris whispers: "Ignore haters." Without gratitude, fans assume selfishness. Without a plan, panic fuels bad tweets. Collapse.

MODERN EPIC SNAPSHOTS

Podcast Host "S."
 Early fame swells. He blasts a critic on Twitter, quote-tweeting their typo. Backlash spirals; sponsors freeze. He logs off for three days, returns with non-apology: "Sorry if you were offended." Downloads crater.

Writer "R."
 Her serial novel misgenders a side character. Readers flag it via feedback form. She thanks them in Sunday thread, commissions a sensitivity reader, and republishes with note: "You caught my blind spot before print." Sales climb; community pride glows. Honor kept, hubris shorn.

CLOSING CALL

> "Thus spoke Achilles, and the Greeks rejoiced to hear
> him,
> for he had put away his rage and turned to battle
> once more."

Your audience does not expect flawlessness; they expect responsiveness. The war for attention is long. Heroes fall, rise, apologize, re-enter the field. Pride makes you potent; humility makes you durable. Weave both. Step forward with spear in hand and ear to ground, ready to charge and ready to kneel.

Chapter 4 – Hephaestus' Shield: World-Building for Brand Depth

"First he forged a shield, great and massive,
plated in bright triple layers.
And on its broad expanse he carved the earth and heavens,
the sea's unwearying waves, the blazing sun and moon,
and all the constellations that crown the vault of night."

Homer pauses the carnage of Book 18 to linger over nine hundred lines of artisanal detail. Achilles is howling for vengeance, yet the poet asks us to marvel at a blacksmith's craft. Why? Because the shield is more than armor. It is a portable universe—farms, cities, dances, feasts, lawsuits, galaxies—layered in concentric rings of meaning. When Achilles strides onto the plain, that cosmos glints on his arm and proclaims, *This warrior carries entire worlds.*

Your brand needs the same depth. Too many creators wave a naked spear—one product, one slogan—while the audience craves a mythic landscape to inhabit. Attention today is not just won; it is homesteaded. Give your followers a shield-world to stroll and they will pitch tents inside your narrative instead of hopping to the next feed. This chapter hands you Hephaestus' blueprint—macro vision etched on the outer ring, recurring series and in-jokes spinning toward the center, and a visual grammar that holds the whole astral map together.

1. The Outer Ring: Macro Vision—Your Mission That Rivets the Cosmos

On the shield's rim Hephaestus places the "great earth, the heavens, and the sea." These are not minor backdrops; they are existential boundaries. Likewise, the outer ring of your brand must declare why this creation matters on a life-sized scale. A macro vision is not a buzz-heavy mission statement buried in an About page. It is the atmosphere every follower inhales the instant they glance at your work.

a. Draft the Cosmic Premise
Answer three prompts in raw sentences:

1. *If your content vanished tonight, what vital human itch would go unscratched tomorrow?*

2. *What injustice or curiosity sits at the root of that itch?*

3. *How does solving it shift culture five years out?*

Distill the trio into one vigorous line, active verb forward. Hephaestus gives us "earth and heaven" in five quick words; keep yours under twelve. Example: "Restore wonder to everyday science."

b. Speak It Everywhere
Carve the line into bios, intros, slide decks, even invoice footers. Repetition turns words into air. Homer repeats "swift-footed

Achilles" more than sixty times; you must echo your macro vision until casual fans can finish the phrase for you.

c. Map Macro to Micro

List every content pillar you publish—videos, threads, guides. Next to each, sketch how it advances or illustrates the macro vision. If a pillar connects only by contortion, drop or re-forge it. The rim of the shield must encircle all else snugly; no dangling continents.

d. Ritualize the Vision

Once a quarter, stage a *Cosmos Campfire*—a livestream or blog post where you revisit the macro line, share evidence of progress, and adjust language if clarity demands. This rhythm signals the cosmos is alive, not static. Achilles' shield is hammered in bronze, but your market breathes.

---

2. The Inner Rings: Recurring Series, Running Jokes, Insider Language

Move inward on the shield and you find contrasting tableaux: a wedding feast beside a courtroom, harvest dances next to besieged cities. These discrete scenes weave a tapestry of human experience and keep the eye roving. Your inner rings do the same with content formats that loop predictably yet feel fresh—serial hooks that bond community.

a. Recurring Series

Series grant structure; the audience knows when to show up and what taste to expect. Examples:

- **Monday Myth-Bust:** Each week you debunk a common misconception in your field.

- **Field-Note Friday:** Share a personal experiment log with wins and flops.

- **30-Second Storyboard:** A micro-video sketch teaching narrative beats.

Craft three series maximum at launch; too many fracture attention. Assign each a distinct tagline and release cadence. Remember Homer's variance: war one ring, peace the next. Balance emotional tones so followers ride a wave, not a drone.

b. Running Jokes

Hephaestus sneaks humor onto the shield: "boys piping, girls in flower-laden dresses." Amid war, life laughs. Running jokes in your brand create insider camaraderie. Perhaps you refer to algorithms as "capricious deities," or every time you mention failure you flash a rubber chicken GIF. The key is consistency plus spontaneity—same joke frame, new situational twist. Fans will quote it back, forging a call-and-response that algorithms can't fabricate.

Rules for running jokes:

1. *Origin Story*: Debut the gag in a memorable post so newcomers can trace lineage.

2. *Consent*: Ensure the humor punches up or inward, never down. Achilles slays, but Homer spares civilians from ridicule.

3. *Evolution*: Let the gag mature. A rubber chicken can wear different hats across seasons.

c. Insider Language

Homeric epithets—"rosy-fingered Dawn," "wine-dark sea"—function as sonic passwords. Listeners know they're inside the story. Develop similar epithets for brand concepts. Rename the comment section "The Agora," call your weekly newsletter "The Forge," label advanced tutorials "Heroic Feats." Drop these terms casually. Newcomers will ask; veterans will answer, initiating them into the guild so you don't have to.

Exercise: Build a micro-lexicon of ten coined phrases. Post it as a pinned resource. Update quarterly as the culture blooms.

---

3. Visual Consistency Checklist—Forging the Shield's Gleam

The shield radiates because its metals and motifs converse. Bronze fades into gold lines that mirror sun on waves. Visual grammar is your quickest trust signal; a stray font is a cracked rivet.

Checklist:

- **Primary Typeface**: One serif or sans-serif for headings, one for body. Choose legibility first, personality second. Achilles' armor is lethal but elegant.

- **Color Trinity**: Pick three hues: base, accent, neutral. Match emotional spectrum to mission—eco brands might pair deep forest green, sunrise orange, off-white.

- **Motif Stamp**: A recurring icon—maybe your initials stylized as a forge hammer, or a minimalist constellation. Insert on thumbnails, slides, corner watermarks.

- **Texture Palette**: Decide on background grain—paper fiber, subtle noise, flat zen garden. Keep it uniform across platforms to mimic the shield's polished field.

- **Photography Treatment**: If you use photos, define a lighting mood (warm dusk, high-key daylight) and stick to it. Random contrast shifts look like sourcing errors, not narrative choice.

- **Motion Rules**: For video intros, limit to one consistent animation style. Hephaestus hammers; he does not sprinkle confetti plus neon lightning plus glitch.

- **Accessibility Scan**: Cross-check color contrasts, caption every audio. A cosmos must be viewable by all eyes and ears.

Audit quarterly. Ask: *Does every asset flash the same heraldic echo?* If not, re-temper in the fire.

---

4. Layer Integration—How the Rings Reinforce Each Other

A universe is not a stack of unrelated slices; gravity locks them. Tie outer and inner rings with visual threads and narrative callbacks.

- When you drop a **Monday Myth-Bust**, preface with the macro vision line: "Restoring wonder to everyday science—today we debunk…"

- Embed insider language into design: the icon for "The Forge" section could be a stylized anvil matching your motif palette.

- Capstone quarterly campfires by expanding the lexicon or evolving a running joke costume, signaling growth.

Think feedback loops: the macro vision powers series topics; series generate language; language shapes visuals; visuals amplify vision. Hephaestus' cosmos whirls but never fragments.

---

5. Expansion Without Dilution—Adding Rings Over Time

In later books Homer will list new heroes, new skirmishes, but the shield remains core. As your brand matures, you may launch a podcast, a course, perhaps a convention. Each is a new ring. Before adding, test:

1. **Alignment**: Does this ring echo the macro vision in theme and tone?

2. **Capacity**: Do you have forge-time to polish it to the visual standards set?

3. **Community Appetite**: Has your audience hinted this layer would enrich their journey?

Prototype with a pilot episode or beta cohort. Gather micro-feedback before engraving the ring in bronze.

---

6. Case Illustrations—Modern Shields in Play

Science YouTuber "Nova"

- Macro vision: "Ignite cosmic awe in classroom minds."

- Series: *Lab Snack* (five-minute micro-experiments), *Teacher-Confessions* (stories of science class fails).

- Running joke: every explosion cue triggers a dancing otter GIF.

- Lexicon: fans are "Star-Kins," merch slogan "Awe Is Fuel."

- Visuals: midnight blue, comet-tail orange, rounded sans-serif.

Outcome: Even casual viewers who land during a trending supernova clip sense the larger universe awaiting subscription.

Finance Writer "Penny Poet"

- Macro vision: "Turn compound interest into everyday art."

- Series: *Haiku Budget*, three-line poems that explain savings hacks.

- Insider language: debt dragons, income rivers.

- Motif: brush-stroke coin icon.

- Running joke: lists mistakes by counting "missed coffee universes" instead of dollars.

Result: Dry numbers morph into mythic creatures readers enjoy slaying each payday.

7. Exercises—Forge Your Brand Shield

Exercise 1: Macro Vision Sprint
 Set timer for ten minutes. Answer the itch-injustice-shift prompts.
Then hammer into a twelve-word vision. Recite aloud until it pings
like bronze—no rattle, pure ring.

Exercise 2: Inner Ring Design Board
 Open a blank digital canvas. Divide into three lanes labeled
Series, Jokes, Lexicon. Brain-storm at least five entries per lane.
Circle the three that energize you most. Schedule pilot drops.

Exercise 3: Visual Audit Walk-Through
 Load your last fifteen posts, slides, or thumbnails into one grid.
Squint. Do they feel like one smith or many vendors? Note stray
colors, fonts, motif gaps. List five immediate fixes. Implement this
week.

---

8. The Shield as Story Artifact—Let Fans Hold the Cosmos

Don't merely display your shield—let the community touch it.
Ideas:

- Publish an interactive map of your lexicon terms with
  Easter-egg tooltips.

- Release PSD or Canva templates using your color trinity
  so fans draft derivative art.

- Host a quarterly *Cosmos Contest*: followers submit meme riffs on running jokes; winners earn custom motif stickers.

Each touchpoint thickens immersion. Your universe becomes co-created, mirroring Homeric oral tradition where listeners shaped tomorrow's performance.

---

9. Watch for Cracks—Maintaining Coherence Under Stress

As Achilles' shield faces spears, yours meets algorithm shifts, burnout, rebrands. Periodically inspect for:

- **Theme Drift** – If new content feels off-topic, revisit the macro line.

- **Visual Rust** – If palettes date or platform dark modes skew tones, refresh but echo core hues.

- **Joke Staleness** – If a gag elicits eye rolls, retire it ceremonially and mint a successor.

Schedule an annual *Forge Day.* Close publishing for 24 hours, review every ring, hammer dents. Post a recap so fans witness stewardship.

Closing Invocation

> "And when the god had finished the starry shield,
> he set it shining before Achilles' mother,
> and she like a hawk glided down to Earth,
> bearing the blaze of a hundred fires."

So you, smith of stories, must finish your shield and send it gleaming into feeds. Followers will carry that blaze, reflecting layers you forged with deliberate care. They will quote lexicon to friends, spot motif signals like constellations, wait for weekly series the way soldiers awaited Dawn's rosy fingers. When a rival brand swings a plain spear, your cosmos will dwarf it—not by force, but by depth. World-building is the quiet gravity that bends all eyes, hearts, and algorithms toward a center of meaning. Hammer true, polish often, and walk onto the digital plain armored in galaxies.

Chapter 5 – Epic Similes: Framing Complex Ideas in Punchy Metaphors

"As a tawny lion, after long famine,
 feels his knees give but still leaps the pens
 to tear a fat ox from its stall—
 so Hector longed to scatter the Argive ranks."

Homer's epic similes give the ear something to chew. They slow the tempo, paint a scene so visceral that when the narrative snaps back to sword-clang we feel the blade land in our own gut. In a world of thumb-scroll speed, your ideas need that same anchoring jolt. A printout of data won't cut it; a flick of metaphor lodges in the cortex.

This chapter is a forge for your own lion-level imagery. You will learn why similes worked for a blind bard on dusty crossroads and why they still magnetize modern feeds. You will build a personal metaphor bank, run the "like vs is" stress test, and craft five hooks ready to deploy in split tests. By the end your language will leap pens, tear dullness from its stall, and feed your audience's imagination until they beg for the next bite.

1 Why the Lion Pounces: The Cognitive Science Behind Epic Simile

Epic similes perform three tasks in one breath:

1. **Compression.** They distill a tangled emotion or procedure into a single snapshot—lion, hunter, storm, bee swarm.

2. **Transfer.** They shift the idea from unfamiliar terrain (bronze tactics, abstract SaaS workflows) to a landscape packed with sensory memory.

3. **Stickiness.** Vivid imagery sparks stronger neural encoding than abstraction. Your brain doesn't store bullet points; it stores pictures that smell of dust and blood.

When Homer compares Achilles to fire "sweeping prairie," every listener has felt heat. That match strike of recognition locks the moment into memory. Translate this to content marketing: your reader has a split-second to decide why they should care. A well-aimed simile turns passive scanning into felt experience.

---

2 Technique Drill: Build a Metaphor Bank

You wouldn't go raiding with an empty quiver. Likewise, you should never sit down to write without a cache of ready images.

Building a metaphor bank is an ongoing habit: observe, record, categorize, retrieve. Follow these phases.

Phase 1: Raw Observation

For seven days carry a pocket notebook or open a rolling note on your phone. Whenever a concrete image slaps your senses—steam curling off pavement, pigeons scrabbling like panicked bookkeepers—jot it. Do not judge relevance. The bank craves volume.

Prompts to spark entries:

- Textures underfoot during your commute.

- Faces in streetlights, coffee froth, skyline gaps.

- Sounds at dawn, when boredom peaks, when adrenaline spikes.

- Smells in elevators, thrift shops, freshwater bays.

Aim for fifty images in a week. The goal is to sharpen the radar, not craft beauty yet.

Phase 2: Categorize Domains

After the week, cluster images by domain. Common buckets:

- **Nature** – storms, rivers, roots.

- **Urban Mechanics** – traffic lights, subways, scaffolds.

- **Human Body** – pulse, breath, scars.

- **Craft & Tool** – anvils, keyboards, bread ovens.

- **Animal Behavior** – pack hunts, moults, migration.

Domain tagging speeds retrieval. When you seek a simile for "rapid iteration," you might flip to Birds and lift "like swifts banking through alley-wind."

Phase 3: Idea-to-Image Mapping

List your core content pillars—maybe productivity, storytelling, ethical finance. Under each pillar, attach three candidate images from the bank. Example: Productivity ↦ potter's wheel spinning, thundercloud rolling across prairie, base drummer locking beat. The mapping trains associative muscles.

Phase 4: Polish & Index

For each mapped pair, write a one-line simile or metaphor. Record both "like" and "is" versions:

- Simile: "Task hand-offs flicker **like** relay batons."

- Metaphor: "Task hand-offs **are** relay batons."

Label tone (gritty, playful) and payload (speed, clarity, urgency) so you grab the right tool later. Store everything in a searchable doc. Congratulations: quiver stocked.

---

3   The "Like vs Is" Test

Epic language toggles between simile ("like") and metaphor ("is"). Each has force; each can overplay its hand. The test is simple:

1. **Draft both forms** for any new image.

2. **Read aloud** each sentence. Listen: Does "like" create distance? Does "is" melt logic?

3. **Apply the Vector Rules.** Use simile when you want a quick flash then back to topic; use metaphor when you want to extend image across multiple beats.

Example Walk-Through

Concept: Onboarding complexity.

- **Simile**: "The new-user flow sprawls **like** an unpruned hedge." (Momentary picture, flow resumes.)

- **Metaphor**: "Your new-user flow **is** an unpruned hedge; every extra click a thicket snagging curious hands." (Invites extended gardening imagery—pruning, sunlight, mulch.)

Test results: If your section ends one sentence later, choose simile. If you plan three paragraphs of horticulture parallels, lock metaphoric mode.

Guardrails:

- Over-extended metaphor feels forced. Exit before the audience senses strain.

- Simile can underwhelm if used for stakes that demand immersion. "War is like a board game" trivializes slaughter. Temper tone.

---

4   Practical Drill: Forging Muscle Memory

Set a thirty-minute daily block for a week. Each day:

1. Select one fresh banking-image pair from the bank.

2. Write a micro-explanation of a core idea (50 words max) using that image twice—once as simile, once as metaphor.

3. Compare tonal shift. Circle the stronger. Archive both.

After seven days you'll have fourteen polished lines and intuitive grasp of "like" vs "is."

5 Five Epic-Simile Content Hooks and A/B Deployment Plan

Below are five ready-to-run hooks for hypothetical topics—feel free to swap nouns to fit your niche. Each hook appears in two variants (A/B). Post A to half your list or alternate days; post B to the other half. Measure open rate or scroll depth. Adopt victors, refine losers.

Hook 1: Overcoming Analysis Paralysis

Variant A (Simile):
 "Your stalled project sits **like** a fortress gate barred from inside—one pin pulled and the whole door swings."

Variant B (Metaphor):
 "Your stalled project **is** a fortress gate barred from inside, obeying a single hidden pin."

Hook 2: Explaining Compound Interest

Variant A:
 "Compound interest grows **like** vine roots—silent, relentless, splitting stone if ignored."

Variant B:
 "Compound interest **is** vine roots, silent yet relentless, splitting stone when neglected."

Hook 3: Describing Agile Sprints

Variant A:
"An agile sprint rolls **like** waves on a breakwater—impact, retreat, leave the wall smoother."

Variant B:
"An agile sprint **is** a wave hitting breakwater, shaping concrete through rhythmic force."

Hook 4: Illustrating Burnout

Variant A:
"Burnout spreads **like** embers under pine-needle carpet—seems out, then leaps into crown fire."

Variant B:
"Burnout **is** an ember buried in pine needles: one gust, and the crown ignites."

Hook 5: Calling for Product-Market Fit

Variant A:
"Searching for product-market fit **is** a blacksmith listening for that single ringing note: any dull thud, back in the forge."

Variant B:
"Product-market fit waits **like** a ringing anvil note—metal sings or you reheat the iron."

Deployment Guide:

- **Platform Split:** If your audience spans newsletter and LinkedIn, run A on one channel, B on the other within same 24-hour window.

- **Metric:** Track click-through or comment quote frequency ("as a vine, wow").

- **Iteration:** After 48 hours, tweak the winning hook for new emoji placement, tense shift, or additional clause; rerun to isolate micro-adjust gains.

---

6   Beyond Hooks: Scaling Epic Simile Across Formats

Hooks lure, but substance keeps. Here's how to propagate metaphor through long-form, video, and talks without exhausting the image.

Long-Form Articles

- **Introduce** with simile quick-flash.

- **Deepen** into metaphor for a mid-section case study.

- **Exit** with callback: transform image to show progress: "The hedge now trimmed, sunlight hits every bud."

Video Essays

- **B-roll Mapping:** If your script says "waves," splice beach footage exactly when word lands.

- **Lower Thirds:** Display key metaphor terms in branded font to imprint subconscious recognition.

Live Workshops

- **Prop Use:** For the blacksmith example, tap a small anvil or metal rod onstage; sound equals sensory seal.

- **Audience Echo:** Ask participants to shout back the image keyword at checkpoints ("Vines!"). Oral tradition reborn.

---

7   Common Pitfalls and Rescue Tactics

1. **Cliché Overload** – "like a well-oiled machine," "busy bees." Use the metaphor bank to dodge worn grooves.

2. **Image-Concept Mismatch** – If your topic is humane design, don't pick predator imagery; cognitive dissonance erodes trust.

3. **Runaway Analogies** – When side-details multiply (sprint team as ship, backlog as barnacles, stakeholders as gulls)

cut back to core before coherence sinks.

Rescue by returning to the bank: find a new domain, simpler object, fresher texture.

---

8   Maintenance: Refreshing the Bank and Measuring Impact

- **Monthly Harvest:** Add ten new images, retire five stale ones.

- **Quarterly Audit:** Pull analytics on posts featuring metaphor vs none. Note dwell time, share count.

- **Annual Festival:** Host a community contest—followers submit their own brand-aligned similes. Reward best with merch or cameo. This crowdsourcing multiplies your bank and deepens communal identity.

Closing Rally

"And just as a falcon, swiftest of all winged things,
   swoops from a height to tear a dove that quivers
below,
   so Achilles fell upon the Trojans."

Homer chooses the falcon not because it is pretty but because its dive matches Achilles' intent—precision and lethal grace. Your metaphors must hunt with that clarity. Build the bank, test like vs is, fire hooks, refine. Soon your ideas will no longer float in abstract ether; they will plunge talon-first into audience memory and feast there long after lesser posts flutter away.

Forge language until imagery sparks. Then carry that spark forward—lion-hungry, falcon-fast, vine-steadfast. The feed is vast, but the mind keeps what roars.

Chapter 6 – Catalogue of Ships: Turning Lists into Momentum Machines

"Now tell me, Muse, the names of captains and their
ships,
 the long-benched vessels that pulled up on Troy's
strand."

Homer interrupts the surge of war to roll out nearly three hundred lines of pure inventory—names, hometowns, hull counts. On the surface the Catalogue of Ships should bore modern ears the way budget tables deaden board meetings. Yet generation after generation sits rapt, letting the cadence of vessels and captains wash over them like drumbeats. The catalogue hypnotizes because it transforms a static list into living momentum. Each entry arrives, stakes its claim, and hands the baton to the next, creating a rhythmic escalation that feels less like data and more like an army marching past the reader's senses.

Creators who master this alchemy can turn any list—features, testimonials, podcast episodes—into a parade that builds anticipation instead of sapping it. This chapter equips you with that skill. You'll learn the structural magic behind Homer's ship roll, see how to sculpt serialized lists that hook followers day after day, use varied pacing to keep the beat fresh, and employ the "Roster Reveal" formula when launching products or seasons. By the time you finish, flat enumerations will become momentum machines that drive clicks, shares, and sustained attention.

1 Why the Catalogue Works: Anatomy of Mesmerizing Lists

Three qualities give Homeric inventory its pull: **identity anchors, rhythmic pulse, and escalating promise.** Understanding them cracks the code for your own content.

1.1 Identity Anchors

Every ship in the catalogue is tied to lineage and locale. "Menestheus brought the Athenians, sons of noble ancestors born in shining Athens." The reader may never visit Athens, but the name sparks homeland pride or curiosity. When you list items, connect each to a persona or purpose so the audience sees more than a bullet—they glimpse story.

1.2 Rhythmic Pulse

Homer drills a formula: hometown—captain—ships, hometown—captain—ships. The chantlike repetition lulls, then the poet breaks it with a sudden flourish—"the swift Myrmidons, where no one yet could equal them in war." The shift jerks attention awake. In digital writing, you mimic this with sentence-length swings, punctuated interruptions, emoji bursts, or media embeds.

1.3 Escalating Promise

The list travels the Greek coast, building the sense of growing force. By the halfway mark the reader feels the shoreline crowded with keels. Your list should likewise accumulate value or excitement, so each entry heightens urgency. Think of a countdown, a rising price ladder, or a skill tree unlocking.

---

2   Series Formats: From Top 10s to Daily Thread Chains

Lists work best when serialized. They reset curiosity at every installment and nudge people back for the next fix. Below are blueprint formats you can adapt.

2.1   Classic Top 10

Structure: Intro framing + entries #10 through #1 + closing flourish.
 Why it works: Reverse ranking builds suspense; readers scan ahead yet linger to confirm expectation.
 Homeric twist: Add lineage snippets. Instead of "Tool #5: Notion," write, "Tool #5, forged in the studios of San Francisco's digital scribes."

2.2   Daily Thread Chain

On platforms like X/Twitter or LinkedIn create a numbered thread: one post per day for a set span—"30 Screenshare Shortcuts in 30 Days." Pin a master index tweet and reply each new item under it. As the thread lengthens, the index accumulates gravity; followers retweet the chain to bookmark.

Implementation tips:

1. Pre-write two weeks ahead so momentum never stalls.

2. Design a visual tile template for each day with slot for title, number, icon—visual unity echoes the coastline of moored ships.

3. Cross-pollinate: convert every seventh post into a short reel or carousel, giving new formats for skimmers.

2.3   Rolling Newsletter Segment

Reserve a sidebar in your newsletter titled "Captain of the Week." Each issue spotlights a sub-topic—API trick, micro-habit, obscure case study. After ten issues, compile entries into a master ebook. This mirrors Homer's gradual march that ultimately forms a single catalogue poem.

---

3   Rhythm & Pacing Tricks: How to Keep Lists Alive

Even the best serial can sag if cadence stagnates. Borrow three metrical tactics from Homer and modern spoken-word poets alike.

3.1   Sentence-Length Waves

Alternate between **long, lulling lines** and **sudden staccato jolts.**
Example:

"Ajax son of Telamon commanded twelve swift vessels trimmed
with scarlet canvas, their bronze prows rising like mountain eagles
ready to swoop.
 Twelve."

The abrupt final word functions as a cymbal hit, resetting attention.
In prose, you might follow a 30-word explanatory sentence with a
two-word punch—"Remember that." Variability keeps cognitive
muscles flexed.

3.2   Pattern Breaks

Every few entries insert a delightful deviation: a GIF, an anecdote,
or a rhetorical question. Homer slips in emotional
commentary—"No archer born could rival Pandarus, if only he had
heeded." Your modern break could be, "Hot take: Number 6 saved
my career, no exaggeration." The surprise oxygenates the scroll.

3.3   Auditory Echoes

Use internal rhyme or alliteration for select lines: "Marcus
marshaled makers of minimalist mock-ups." The aural bounce
ensures recall. Employ sparingly to avoid sing-song overload.

4   The "Roster Reveal" Formula for Product Launches

Launching a new course, community, or SaaS feature set? Treat it like mustering ships. Names, specs, purpose—rolled out in a tempo that snowballs excitement.

Stage 1: Whisper Tease (T-30 to T-21 days)

Hint at numbers without details. "Thirty keels gather in the fog." Post blurred mock-ups, silhouette GIFs, or cryptic emojis. Goal: spark speculation threads.

Stage 2: First Wave (T-20 to T-15)

Reveal 20 % of the lineup—your "Locrian ships." Give each a title card: name, flagship feature, origin story in one sentence. Encourage followers to guess what's next.

Stage 3: Mid-Roll Surge (T-14 to T-7)

Drop daily reveals. Use rhythm tricks: long caption + one-word punch. Tie each entry to a use-case persona so prospects self-identify. Offer a limited-time bonus for early adopters who commit before full roster public.

Stage 4: Penultimate Break (T-6 to T-3)

Pause reveals. Instead publish behind-the-forge footage—UX sketches, blooper reels, team huddles. This gap heightens craving like Homer's aside before his catalogue resumes.

Stage 5: Grand Muster (Launch Day)

Post the full roster in cascading thread or scrolling landing page. Start big—"Like a line of black-prowed galleys, thirty tools stand ready"—then march through each entry with polished tiles linking to feature docs. Close with a CTA echoing the initial tease: "The fog lifts. Choose your vessel."

Stage 6: After-Action Echo (Week +1)

Publish a retrospective "Tally of Keels" thanking early users by handle, sharing first stats, and teasing expansions ("new allies sail at midsummer"). This cements belonging and signals ongoing voyage.

---

5 Case Illustration: A Fictional Creator Puts It All Together

Scenario: "OrbitFrame," a software studio, plans to launch a suite of 12 tactical AI-assist browser extensions for designers.

- **Tease:** They tweet a starry GIF captioned "12 lights flicker beyond the horizon."

- **First Wave:** Reveal extensions 1–3 with cosmic-themed art. Designer chatter explodes on Slack groups guessing tools #4–#12.

- **Daily Drip:** One thread per day. Sentences vary: "Nebula Sketch brings color palettes faster than dawn." Next tweet: "Speed."

- **Pattern Break:** Day 7 features a video call where devs share "sleep-deprived patch notes," humanizing myth.

- **Roster Reveal:** Landing page lists all 12 under "The Constellation," each with scroll-triggered glow animation.

- **Echo:** A week later, OrbitFrame emails "Tally of Orbits," highlighting top 3 user-generated projects and promising "two new satellites" before fall. Sign-ups double.

---

6 Exercises: Your Turn to Muster

Exercise 1: List Remix Drill

Pick a dull spreadsheet—expense categories, CRM lead statuses, academic sources. Rewrite as a catalogue of ships. Name each entry, give an origin, insert a rhythmic break every fifth line. Read aloud. Notice how sonic variance rescues tedium.

Exercise 2: Serial Blueprint

Sketch a 14-day thread chain for your domain. Define daily titles, emoji icons, and which three days will house pattern-break media. Pre-record or outline content; load draft posts into scheduler.

Exercise 3: Roster Simulation

Draft a mini-launch of five offerings (could be blog post series,
mini-products). Follow the Roster Reveal timeline in compressed
form—whisper tease now, first wave tomorrow, full muster three
days out. Track mention rates and open loops in comments.

7 Potential Pitfalls and How to Navigate

1. **List Fatigue:** If engagement dips mid-series, inject an
   unexpected guest voice or merge two entries into a combo
   drop.

2. **Reveal Spoilers:** Over-eager fans might leak full roster.
   Lean in—confirm leak but add new twist ("You saw the
   keels, but not the sea-monster upgrade!").

3. **Cadence Slip:** Vacation, illness, tech glitches. Have two
   buffer entries prepped. If you still miss, own it publicly and
   offer a make-good bonus. Achilles rebukes Agamemnon
   openly; honesty retains honor.

8 Beyond Words: Multisensory Lists

- **Audio Lists:** Record an ASMR-style whisper naming each ship/tool with subtle hull-creak sound bed.

- **Interactive Maps:** Build a clickable coastline where each moored ship icon reveals an entry.

- **Physical Artefacts:** Limited posters listing top community contributors in bronzed lettering mailed to superfans.

Every new medium grafted onto the list extends its lifespan and widens emotional reach.

Closing Charge

> "And the ships, drawn up line on line,
>   shone like teeth of a serried saw beneath the dawn."

Your lists can gleam the same way—each item a tooth catching morning light, the whole row suggesting unstoppable forward cut. Whether you count down books, unveil software modules, or parade testimonial screenshots, use identity anchors, rhythmic pulse, and escalating promise to turn enumeration into exhilaration. Muster your fleet, vary your beats, and launch down the algorithmic strait with the sea-spray of momentum foaming at your prow. The audience will watch, spellbound, until the last hull vanishes into the sunrise—and they will scroll tomorrow hoping to see more sails.

Chapter 7 – The Duel Scene: One-to-One Engagement at Scale

"And all the Trojans and Achaeans sat still upon their shields,
 spears planted, while in the clear ground between the armies
 Paris and Menelaus squared to fight for Helen's love."

The *Iliad* pivots on a single combat that pauses the clash of nations. Paris steps forward in gleaming mail, Menelaus strides out roaring challenge, and two vast hosts freeze—tens of thousands transfixed by one narrow patch of turf. The duel concentrates narrative electricity. It funnels sprawling conflict into a focus so sharp every heartbeat thuds louder, every breath stalls. Homer knows: if you want a multitude to care at once, pit two vivid personalities against each other in full public view.

As a content creator, you rarely command nations, but platforms give you digital plains where thousands graze their feeds. A one-to-one engagement—debate, interview, live critique—can slice through scroll fatigue the way bronze edges silk. Done right, it turns lurkers into active witnesses, then subscribers, then evangelists. This chapter shows how to stage that duel, broadcast it, and harvest the momentum long after spears clatter to earth.

1 Why Paris vs Menelaus Magnets Attention

Three forces lock eyes on the duel: **stakes, intimacy, and spectacle.**

Stakes—Menelaus fights to reclaim a stolen queen; Paris fights to keep honor and life. The outcome could end—or ignite—the war. Your event needs equivalent weight: solve an urgent question, crown a champion idea, settle a rivalry the audience already gossips about.

Intimacy—suddenly every viewer can track the micro-expressions of two faces. In feeds, intimacy appears when a live cam zooms close, when two creators banter unscripted, when chat queries receive names.

Spectacle—the armies form a living arena, shields glitter, priests pour wine, but all embellishment frames the duel's center. Modern spectacle is crisp lighting, on-screen overlays, poll bars climbing in real time, remix chains sprouting across platforms.

Anchor your plan on these pillars. Then forge tactics worthy of Homer's heralds.

2 Strategy: Schedule Public Debates and AMA Showdowns

2.1 Choose the Combatants

- **Icon vs Icon** – two respected voices with opposing takes. The audience tunes in expecting wit and parity.

- **Mentor vs Protégé** – showcase growth, model respectful push-back.

- **Creator vs Community** – AMA where followers pose unfiltered challenges.

Compatibility matters: both must share enough domain overlap for a coherent clash but differ enough to spark friction. Vet tone, language, and boundaries first; you want heat, not hate.

2.2 Cast the Heralds

In Homer, a herald walks the line, announcing rules and swearing oaths. Online, a *moderator* and a *producer* play those roles. The moderator enforces time, protects civility, and clarifies tangents. The producer handles tech and cues overlays. Draft a cue sheet: intro – bio beats – challenge round – audience volley – closing pledges. Share it three days ahead so everyone sharpens arguments rather than fumbles logistics.

2.3   Set the Truce and the Turf

The duel occurs in a neutral no-man's-land. Your turf might be:

- A Twitter/X Spaces room.

- A YouTube co-stream using split-screen.

- An Instagram Live where hosts trade control.

- A Discord Stage with chat muted until Q&A.

Declare ground rules publicly: time boxes, language guardrails, ban on personal insults. A visible truce reassures onlookers they can watch without dread scroll.

2.4   Pre-Battle Pageantry

Menelaus arms himself in bright bronze; Paris perfumes his hair. Pageantry builds suspense. Announce the duel at least one week ahead:

- Post side-by-side promo art: two avatars glaring.

- Drop a countdown widget on stories.

- Encourage fans to submit opening questions tagged with a unique hashtag—"#ShieldClash."

Pin a trailer to your profile: thirty-second montage of previous zingers, stats flashing like burnished greaves. The goal is to turn casual feed walkers into ticket holders.

2.5 Run of Show

1. **Ceremonial Oath (2 min):** Moderator frames stakes.

2. **Opening Blades (5 min each):** Each combatant states thesis undisturbed.

3. **Crossfire Rounds (3 × 6 min):** Timed rebuttals.

4. **Audience Volley (15 min):** Rapid-fire questions streamed from poll top-votes or voice queue.

5. **Shield-Drop Summaries (2 min each):** Combatants end with one actionable takeaway.

6. **Call to Campfires (2 min):** Moderator directs spectators to specific subscription points—newsletter, discord, replay link.

Time discipline matters. Overrun and you squander urgency; end right at crescendo and chat begs for encore.

2.6 After-Action exploits

- **Highlight Reel** within three hours—clip the sharpest thirty seconds, caption it, post cross-platform.

- **Transcript with Commentary** inside twenty-four hours—publish on blog, sprinkle timestamp anchors, embed subscription boxes every 600 words.

- **Opinion Poll Follow-up** at forty-eight hours—"Who persuaded you?" Share results, tease next duel.

These echoes extend half-life. Paris and Menelaus fight once, but bards recount for centuries; your replay should echo at least a fortnight.

---

3   Tools: Polls, Duets, Stitched Reactions—Turning Spectators into Subscribers

3.1   Real-Time Polls

While hosts spar, pin a poll asking whose argument currently resonates. Updating bars gamify viewership—each vote a micro-pledge. End poll when event ends; screenshot final tally; share in recap newsletter with signup CTA: "Join here to steer the next debate."

Platforms:

- YouTube Live: built-in poll widget.

- Twitter Spaces: use companion tweet polls.

- Twitch: chat-integrated poll pop-ups.

3.2   Duets & Remixes

On TikTok or Instagram Reels, fans can split-screen your clip and add commentary—echoes multiplying noise. Post a short excerpt marked "Duet this argument if you dare." Provide a trending audio bed. Each duet displays your handle; algorithm funnels curious new watchers back to origin.

To prime, release a 15-second vertical bite: combatant declares a bold stat; leave a beat of silence. That pause invites a reaction.

3.3   Stitched Reactions

YouTube Shorts "remix," X/Twitter Quote reposts, or LinkedIn stitched articles let influencers clip your duel and append perspective. Encourage with open license: "Feel free to stitch, just tag us and #ShieldClash." Set up a brand monitor to retweet best stitches, rewarding the loop.

3.4   Conversion Scaffold

Every spectator impulse must have a catch-net:

1. **Pinned Landing Page**: banner with duel replay, bullet summary, signup form, next event calendar.

2. **Chat Bots**: auto-respond to "/subscribe" cue during live chat.

3. **Overlay QR Codes**: full-screen flicker mid-show; watchers scan, drop email, rejoin within seconds.

4. **Guest Discount Codes**: each combatant offers exclusive perk—ebook, template—redeemable only by subscribers within 24 hours. Scarcity converts fence-sitters.

3.5 Analytics Loop

Track:

- Peak concurrent viewers vs baseline content.

- Chat messages per minute.

- Post-event subscriber surge.

- Replay completion rate.

Graph these across duels. Identify matchup types and time slots that spike conversions. Adjust future scheduling like generals adjusting phalanx after skirmish recon.

4 Crafting the Duel Narrative: A Storyboard Framework

Even spontaneous brawls outline themselves in arcs. Draft a storyboard akin to three-act play:

- **Act I – Challenge Thrown:** Why must this duel happen now? Hook feed browsers with a flashpoint anecdote.

- **Act II – Clash of Steel:** Structured argument exchange. Crescendo at midpoint; introduce surprise data or third-party clip.

- **Act III – Aftermath & Invitation:** Cool-down reflection plus marching orders: download guide, vote on next topic, share highlight.

Storyboard keeps you from meandering, and it signals to habitual watchers that your events deliver closure.

---

5 Building a Duel-Ready Audience Ecosystem

One spectacle cannot hold eternity. Create a layered ecosystem so duel watchers slide into deeper trenches of your brand.

5.1   Outer Rim – Casual Observers

They catch highlight clips via hashtags. Feed them snackable context threads and annotated pull quotes. CTA: "Follow for the next clash."

5.2   Middle Ring – Active Commenters

These join live, vote in polls, clip duets. Offer them a free mini-course or resource vault unlocked via email. Give badges or flair in chat: *Shield-Bearer*. Recognize them publicly at the start of every stream.

5.3   Inner Citadel – Core Strategists

Hardcore fans who analyze arguments, suggest matchmaking, volunteer moderating. Invite them to a closed Discord or Circle community. Monthly planning calls let them preview upcoming rosters and propose weapons (topics). This fosters co-ownership; they recruit friends to strengthen their faction.

The funnel mirrors Homeric society: onlookers, rank-and-file soldiers, generals advising kings.

---

6   Case Study Composite: Turning a Debate into 10k Subscribers

Imagine "Design Duel," a YouTube channel hosting head-to-head UX critiques. They schedule "Figma vs Pen-and-Paper: Which sparks better wireframes?" Combatants: a tool evangelist and a handmade-purist.

Pre-Battle: Trailer drops Monday. Twitter poll asks, "Which side are you on?" 3k votes. Newsletter provides a bracket graphic; readers guess winner for sticker pack.

Live: 6 pm Friday. 4k live viewers, polls every ten minutes, overlay timer. Chat commands: "!figma" pops trial link; "!paper" pops discount code for artisanal notebooks.

Post: Saturday morning highlight reel hits shorts; one clip hits 200k views on Reels. Landing page offers replay transcript plus duel cheat sheet. 10k new emails within 72 hours, 61 % from remix traffic.

Snowball: Community votes next clash: "AI Mockup vs Human Flair." Brand momentum mounts—each duel a thunderclap, each thunderclap swelling the army.

---

7 Advanced Tactics and Variations

7.1 Triangular Showdowns

Add a third debater midway to shift alliances—echoes the gods tilting duels with sudden divine thrusts. Warn audience beforehand to guess surprise entrant for bonus points.

7.2 Silent Round

Mid-duel, require combatants to present a slide deck while mute; audience interprets visuals in chat. Engagement spikes as viewers co-create meaning.

7.3 Redemption Arcs

Loser of last duel returns armed with new data. Nothing rivets like a comeback narrative—think Hector rallying after early setbacks.

---

8 Handling Collateral Damage: Moderating Conflict and Backlash

Homer shows even duels can trigger chaos: an arrow later breaks truce. Your digital arena might erupt with trolls or off-topic spam. Arm up:

- **Slow Mode Chat** after toxic spikes.

- **Shadow Bans** for slurs or doxing.

- **Moderator Signal Phrases** ("Red Shield") to pause stream if lines cross.

Post-event, publish community guideline reminders. A public code of honor allows strong debates without scorched trust.

9   Exercises: Forge Your Duel Playbook

1. **Identify Foes or Foils:** List five creators with contrasting views; score mutual respect potential.

2. **Draft a 90-Second Trailer:** Write script and shot list; rehearse voiceover to ensure tension and clarity.

3. **Create Poll Ladder:** Design three polls escalating difficulty, to run pre-live, during live, after live.

4. **Sketch Conversion Landing Page:** Headline, reel embed, three bullet summary, single email form, next duel schedule.

5. **Mock Post-Mortem Report Template:** Sections for peaks, chat sentiment, subscriber delta—fill after first duel.

Repeat cycle until muscle memory locks in.

Closing Call

"Thus spoke Hector of the flashing helm, and the armies rejoiced,

for the fight would fix the quarrel of years in one short
hour."

Your duel may last thirty minutes, but in that crucible you forge
loyalty faster than months of isolated monologue. A well-staged
clash crystallizes ideas, focuses collective gaze, and opens back
doors for thousands to march from spectator hill into your fortified
community. Parse lessons from Paris and Menelaus: clear stakes,
tight rules, vivid storytelling. Schedule your debate, sharpen your
stance, polish polls, ready the remix field. When the signal horn
blares—go live, face to face—armies of cursors will halt and
watch. Then guide them, still pulsing, toward the subscription
gates, as dawn's rosy fingers brighten new horizons in your
growing digital kingdom.

Chapter 8 – Rallying the Achaeans: Story Arcs that Retain Attention

"Then the lord of men, wide-ruling Agamemnon,
sprang to his feet and cried aloud:
'Friends, Achaean heroes, not yet look for flight!
One speech, one charge, and victory is ours.'"

A thousand throats had begun to murmur retreat. Hector's onslaught smashed the Greek wall, and the surf of panic foamed up the beach. At that hour Agamemnon did what only a leader can do: he told a story of what would happen *if* they stood, *if* they broke, and *how* dawn would paint their triumph if courage held another hour. His words moved warriors more than bronze. Homer shows that storytelling, not shouting, stabilizes morale. The king shoves his men into a three-beat arc—present dread, looming consequence, promised renewal—and the line holds.

Digital audiences waver the same way. Followers scan feeds, wincing at doomscroll headlines, ready to bail on your tutorial or product preview at any lull. A weekly content arc, shaped like Agamemnon's speech—*tension, consequence, renewal*—turns passive subscribers into return readers who crave the next beat. This chapter dissects the cycle, then guides you in storyboarding three-episode mini-sagas that teach product skills while fueling cliffhanger anticipation.

1 Why Morale Speeches Work: Neuroscience of Suspense and Resolution

When Agamemnon paints the dire image—"walls aflame, wives enslaved"—the soldiers' cortisol spikes. He immediately sketches the opposite future—"ships crowned with trophies, bards singing your names"—and dopamine glimmers. The *gap* between dread and hope is tension; the *bridge* is action. Human brains wire for tension-bridge payoffs. A story arc harnesses that circuitry.

In weekly content, tension is the unsolved pain, consequence is what worsens if inertia holds, renewal is the transformation your product enables. Deliver each beat across consecutive drops, and you replicate the hormonal roller-coaster that kept hoplites kneeling to the king's rally instead of sprinting for the surf.

---

2 Framework: The Tension–Consequence–Renewal Cycle

Visualize a three-paned shield: left gouge, center crack, right freshly forged gleam. Each pane equals one weekly episode.

2.1 Episode 1 – Tension (The Crack Appears)

Purpose: awaken pain. Show the audience a scenario rattling their current comfort.

Structure:

1. **Inciting Moment** – a data point or anecdote.

2. **Emotional Mirror** – "You feel the jolt, don't you?"

3. **Open Loop** – "Next week I'll show how this crack widens unless…"

Tone: urgent yet restrained; no fixes. Leave minds twitching.

2.2 Episode 2 – Consequence (The Crack Widens)

Purpose: escalate stakes. Demonstrate cost of inaction.

Structure:

1. **Recap** – one-sentence flashback.

2. **Deep Dive** – stats, case study, villain exposition.

3. **Pressure Valve** – hint at possible remedy: "There *is* a forge that mends."

Tone: darker, factual. You're Agamemnon pointing at burning huts.

2.3 Episode 3 – Renewal (The Shield Reforged)

Purpose: deliver solution. Walk audience through transformation, equip with first actionable step.

Structure:

1. **Before/After Image** – vivid snapshot of repaired future.

2. **Forge Walkthrough** – product feature or process demo.

3. **Forward Promise** – workbook, webinar, next saga tease.

Tone: uplifting, directive. End with call to march.

---

3 Practice: Storyboard Three-Episode Mini-Sagas Around Product Education

Below are three sample sagas for a hypothetical SaaS called *TaskForge*: a project-management tool aimed at freelance teams. Adapt shapes and timings to your own arena.

Saga A – "The Lost Invoice" (teaches automated billing)

Episode 1 – Tension: "The Inbox Ambush"

Inciting Moment: You wake to twenty color-coded email flags—payment overdue memes from clients.
Emotional Mirror: "Ever sworn a spreadsheet vow at 2 a.m.?"
Open Loop: "Next Thursday we'll watch that vow snap."

Episode 2 – Consequence: "Domino Debt"

Recap: "Remember Monday's inbox ambush."
 Deep Dive: Chart—late invoice cascades into credit-card interest, missed rent.
 Pressure Valve: "A single toggle could disarm the ambush."

Episode 3 – Renewal: "Forge Your Auto-Anvil"

Before/After: Side-by-side of clogged inbox vs auto-sent PDF with confetti emoji, paid stamp.
 Forge Walkthrough: Screen share—set trigger, personalize template, schedule recurring.
 Forward Promise: Download checklist; next saga: scope creep slayer.

Saga B – "The Vanishing Brief" (teaches project template library)

Episode 1 – Tension: "Client's Blank Stare"

Designer meets client; brief evaporates into shrug.
 Loop: "Week's end we watch a dozen hours vanish."

Episode 2 – Consequence: "Hourglass Blood-letting"

Breakdown of time wasted reinventing doc. Show timer GIF bleeding sand.
 Pressure: "There is a shelf of blueprints hidden in plain sight."

Episode 3 – Renewal: "Template Vault Break-in"

Show TaskForge library; duplicate template; link to custom fields.
Call: import one today; next saga: feedback labyrinth escape.

Saga C – "The Discord Inferno" (teaches comment aggregation panel)

Episode 1 tension: frantic ping swarm.
Episode 2 consequence: screenshot of five platforms, contradictory feedback, project derail.
Episode 3 renewal: unify streams into TaskForge panel; color code; filter by priority.

---

4 Creating Your Own Mini-Saga—Step-By-Step

1. **Define One Learning Outcome.** What single user ability must rise by episode three?

2. **List Pain Signals.** Collect three sentences your audience says when struggling with that ability. Choose the rawest for episode-one inciting line.

3. **Quantify Consequence.** Find a statistic or narrative of failure. Exaggeration okay if sourced. Insert chart or metaphor for visceral effect.

4. **Map Product Feature to Solution.** Identify which UI path relieves the pain fastest; script a screen walkthrough.

5. **Design Cliffhangers.** Episode one ends with question; episode two ends with tease: "Tomorrow I reveal the two-click hack."

6. **Build Visual Cohesion.** Use consistent thumbnail motif, perhaps cracked shield gradually mending.

7. **Schedule and Tease.** Publish episode one Monday morning; teaser for two lands in stories Monday night; episode two Wednesday; episode three Friday—week sealed.

---

5 Rhythm, Cadence, Breath—Oral Roots Meet Algorithms

Agamemnon doesn't read from a tablet; he rides cadence: long rolling vow, short barked command. Mimic in prose:

- **Episode Openers:** start with a one-beat exclamation—"Listen." "Look."

- **Pulse Sentences:** alternate 20-word picture lines with 3-word hammer lines.

- **Chorus Tags:** repeat a phrase across all three installments—"Hold the line." Audiences grip familiarity.

Algorithms favor dwell time; cadence sustains eyes.

---

6 Measuring Retention and Refinement

Track:

- Episode drop-off: percent who finish first vs third post.

- Click-through to product demo.

- Reply volume containing saga chorus tag.

If retention sags between episode two and three, tighten consequence section or shorten interval to one day instead of two. Iterate.

---

7   Expansion: Parallel Arcs and Seasonal Campaigns

Once you master one three-episode mini-saga, run two in parallel aimed at different personas—rookie, pro. Later knit six sagas into a quarterly "campaign epic." Conclude with a live Q&A (see Chapter 7) where you recap arcs, award "Hero of the Sprint" badges, and pitch premium tiers.

---

8   Exercises

1. **Write a Hero Speech.** Draft 150 words using tension–consequence–renewal to rally your list toward adopting a neglected feature.

2. **Storyboard Grid.** Sketch thumbnails for three episodes; write five-word working titles; pin on Trello.

3. **Cliffhanger Workshop.** Compose three closing lines, each ending with question, statistic droplet, or emotional promise. Read aloud, choose most magnetic.

Practice until beats ring like steel on helm.

Closing Invocation

> "Their hearts leapt hearing the king's cry;
> spears shook, shields sang; no man dreamt of
> fleeing."

Muster your followers the same. Carve tension until hearts race, lay out consequence until minds dread stagnation, then blaze renewal so bright action feels inevitable. Weekly arcs executed with Agamemnon's timing will keep your Achaeans—users, readers, students—at the ramparts, eager for next dawn's sortie. Hold the line, tell the tale, and victory—retention—will be yours.

Chapter 9 – Trojan Horse Tactics: Collaboration & Guest Appearances

"They hollowed out the belly, laid bare the ribs of timber,
 and inside that dark hold picked men of Greece sat armed,
 waiting for night to loose them on unwary Troy."

For ten stubborn years the Greeks hurled bronze and brawn against Troy's ramparts. Battering failed. Negotiation failed. But a shift in strategy—an apparently harmless gift—tipped a stalemate into conquest. The Trojan Horse is more than lore; it is the founding case study on embedding value inside a vessel your target is eager to pull inside the gate. In the creator economy, collaboration is that vessel. Guest threads, joint livestreams, and free templates slip past skepticism, expose you to warm audiences, and expand territory faster than solo sieges.

This chapter drills a Trojan Horse playbook: how to scout complementary creators (audience overlap below thirty percent so expansion, not cannibalization, occurs), how to hammer together co-produced assets that look like gifts while hiding mutual influence, and how to guide new arrivals through a nurture funnel until they pledge loyalty to your newsletter, podcast, or product. When we are done you will craft partnerships that Trojan brass would envy—quiet on the outside, explosive in impact.

1 Why the Horse Worked: Psychology of Accepted Gifts

Before timber groaned through Troy's gates, a rumor paved the way: the horse was a peace offering to Athena. Gift framing flipped Trojan mindsets from defense to desire. Modern audiences behave similarly. When two creators drop a co-branded freebie or host an unpaywalled conversation, walls lower. Reciprocity bias nudges people toward exploration rather than suspicion. The collaborator's endorsement acts as social proof; your expertise rides piggyback.

Key insight: influence hidden inside value feels earned, not advertised.

---

2 Playbook Step One: Identify Complementary Creators (Overlap < 30 Percent)

> "Odysseus chose the keenest hearts in all the host,
> men skilled in every craft of silent war."

2.1 Define Your Core and Adjacent Domains

List your main content pillars—say, "email copy," "freelance pricing," "creator mindset." Now map adjacent but distinct domains where a partner could reign—"cold-outreach design," "small-biz legal," "burnout psychology." Complement means audiences share values but not redundant content.

2.2 Quantify Overlap

- **Metric A: Audience Intersection** – Use social-media analytics or manual sampling. If 10 percent of your newsletter subscribers also open the potential partner's emails, you are safe. If 40 percent appear in both, risk cannibalizing.

- **Metric B: Value Delta** – How far does their promise stretch beyond yours? The greater the delta, the greater curiosity your collab stirs.

2.3 Vetting Filters

1. **Reputation Alignment** – Honor counts. A single shady co-sign can torch years of trust.

2. **Production Standards** – Mismatched audio, sloppy slides signal amateurism.

3. **Reciprocation Capacity** – They must have bandwidth and incentives to promote.

Create a short-list of five. Rank by Delta×Capacity. Now prepare approach letters.

3 Playbook Step Two: Co-Create Trojan Assets

"In that vast horse they sat,
 gripping spears, hearts beating under hammered helms,
 while Greek fires dwindled on the shore—a ruse to lure the foe."

The asset must look like a windfall for the recipient audience yet contain chambers that carry each creator's brand deeper.

3.1 Asset Archetypes

a. Freebie Templates

- *Design:* Branded universally—logos discreet, but color palette invokes each creator.

- *Structure:* Intro sheet (co-story), main worksheet, bonus tab linking to deeper resources behind email opt-in.

- *Hidden Influence:* Tutorial video accessible via QR in sheet, cross-upsells your premium course.

b. Joint Livestreams

- *Format:* 40-minute deep-dive, 10-minute Q&A.

- *Stagecraft:* Split-screen overlays show both handles; slide deck alternates voices every three slides to avoid dominance.

- *Hidden Influence:* At the halfway mark drop a challenge with downloadable guide only accessible via dual-opt-in form.

c. Micro-eBooks

- *Theme:* Hybrid niche—e.g., "Legal Loopholes That Double Cold-Email Conversion."

- *Design:* Two voices in alternating sidebars, fostering dialogue vibe.

- *Hidden Influence:* Final page "Take the Siege Further" lists upcoming webinars—each host leads one.

d. Crossover Podcast Series
Three episodes: Host A interviews B, B interviews A, final roundtable with audience call-ins. Convert audio to text; embed clip quotations for SEO.

3.2   Gift-First Copywriting

Headline must scream benefit, not brand. "The No-Stress Pricing Sheet" outranks "Collab: Acme & Beta Webinar." In Trojan terms, wood grain hides iron.

3.3 Operational Logistics

- **Asset Timeline** – two-week outline, one-week production, three-day QA.

- **File Handoff** – central shared folder, version tags.

- **Distribution Date Sync** – unify clocks; surprise requires simultaneous gate opening.

---

4 Playbook Step Three: The Post-Collab Nurture Funnel

The gate slams. What next? Greeks burned Troy because infantry poured out of the belly immediately; not months later.

4.1 Day-Zero Warm Welcome

As opt-ins flow, trigger an email:
 "Subject: ⚔ Found you via the Horse—welcome to camp!"
 Inside: mini-roadmap of value, personal origin anecdote, zero ask.

4.2 Day-Two Quick Win

Send actionable micro-tip using the collab asset. Eg: "Line 14 of the Pricing Sheet auto-calculates margin—here's how to tweak."

Prompt reply with screenshot of their tweak; this sparks conversation loop.

4.3 Day-Five Authority Story

Share a result case: "Designer Lara shaved six hours after template." Link to in-depth article. Now trust is cementing; position premium product soft mention.

4.4 Day-Seven Invitation to Deeper Circle

Offer live Q&A for new cohort. Co-host returns briefly—reinforce alliance credibility. Push sign-up to your community plan or course wait-list.

4.5 Segmenting and Retargeting

Tag leads by engagement heat. Use pixel retarget ads showcasing next-level product. Those who clicked case study but skipped Q&A receive gentle nudge—"Missed the campfire? Catch replay."

4.6 Long-Arc Retention

At week four, survey: what new struggle surfaced after using asset? Use answers to plan next Trojan initiative, looping cycle.

5 Worked Example: The "Quiet Marketer" & "Data Bard"

5.1 Scouting

Quiet Marketer (QM) teaches introverts social-media strategy. Data Bard (DB) visualizes analytics artfully. Overlap survey shows 22 percent. Complement passed.

5.2 Asset

Title: "Silent Signals – a template that turns numbers into non-talky content prompts."
 PDF with Google Sheets link. Hidden chamber: optional script that pulls user's analytics and suggests post themes—requires both creators' APIs.

5.3 Launch Sequence

- Teaser reels on both channels: silent film style captions summarizing problem.

- Day of drop: countdown tweets, link blast to Typeform gate.

- 4,400 opt-ins first 48 hrs.

5.4   Funnel Performance

- 60 percent open Day-Zero email.

- 900 attend Q&A.

- 310 purchase QM's self-paced course; 95 subscribe to DB's dashboard SaaS at founder discount.

Joint revenue: $38k in ten days, plus list growth for each >3k.

---

6   Advanced Trojan Variants

6.1   Nested Horses

Hide a mini-gift inside the first. Example: the free template contains secret link to Easter-egg Notion hub; those who find it get early-bird to next collab. Gamified intrigue deepens belonging.

6.2   Third-Party "Priest" Endorsements

Remember Trojans wheeled the horse partly because a priest misread omens. Secure a respected curator (newsletter research, industry journalist) to introduce your collab, stamping neutrality.

6.3   Localization Horses

Translate asset into three languages; recruit micro-influencers native to each. Expansion multiplies without overexposing core lists.

6.4   Timed Detonations

Set asset to unlock premium chapter two weeks after download. Pushes sustained engagement; algorithm values returning visitors.

---

7   Pitfalls and Counter-Measures

1. **Mismatch of Work Ethic** – one creator delays, damages trust. Solution: draft collaboration charter with deadlines, fallback kill-switch.

2. **Audience Whiplash** – if voice styles clash, pre-record a banter intro bridging vibes.

3. **Saturation** – too many collabs dilute uniqueness. Cap at two Trojan drops per quarter.

---

8   Exercises

1. **Overlap Audit:** open spreadsheet, list ten potential partners. Gather audience size and shared follower % via sample poll. Highlight cells <30 percent.

2. **Horse Blueprint:** draft one-page brief of asset—goal, deliverable, hidden influence path, timeline.

3. **Nurture Flow Map:** sketch seven-day email ladder, assign objective and micro-CTA to each.

4. **Post-Mortem Template:** create doc for metrics capture—opt-ins, CTR, revenue, unsubscribes. Use after each collab to guide iteration.

Closing Rally

> "Thus, by their own hands, the Trojans hauled doom within their gates,
> and in that hushed night the hidden Greeks rose,
> flung wide the doors, and let the future rush in on clattering feet."

Collaboration, when designed as a Trojan Horse, lets you stride into cities of attention that stonewalled solo thrusts. Identify allies whose realms complement yours, craft gifts so irresistible gatekeepers beg to ferry them inside, and stand ready with nurture fires once the doors swing wide. Do this and your influence will multiply noiselessly until sunrise reveals banners flying from towers thought impossible yesterday. Soldiers win battles; strategists win wars. Choose your wood, choose your crew, and roll.

Chapter 10 – Olympian Politics: Understanding Platform Biases

"Now Zeus the Cloud-Gatherer tipped his golden
scales;
 in one dish he placed the Greeks' day of glory,
 in the other, Trojan doom, and the beam sank toward
Ilium."

Homer refuses to paint war as a meritocracy. Achilles may be unstoppable, Hector may burn with duty, yet neither decides the battle alone. The gods brood above, whisper into winds, slide weights onto cosmic balances. Zeus favors one side, then—prodded by Hera or Thetis—nudges fortune back. Every fighter on the plain must factor divine mood into strategy.

Digital creators face similar meteorology. Platforms—YouTube, Instagram, TikTok, X, LinkedIn, Substack, Medium—are not neutral bulletin boards. They are Olympian courts with creaking levers and shifting edicts executed by code. One day short-form loops vault ordinary dancers to stardom; next week long-form analysis wins the algorithmic laurel. If you ignore these undercurrents you become Hector praying to an absent Apollo. If you learn their pattern, you glide in tailwinds others mistake for luck.

This chapter demystifies platform politics. You will dissect ranking levers on major networks, discover how to read weather signs, and set up a quarterly "Divine Favor Audit" that tracks feature shifts like augurs watching bird flights. Your goal is not slavish appeasement but informed adaptation—craft that speaks with your voice while riding the thermals Zeus already blows.

---

1   The Lesson: Zeus Tips Scales; Platforms Aren't Neutral

Algorithms pursue corporate objectives: watch-time, ad inventory, subscription retention, market expansion. They privilege behaviors that meet those targets—even if official blog posts preach neutrality.

On YouTube, "time watched per session" reigns; quick exits damage ranking. Instagram privileges fresh audiovisual hybrids—Reels over static photos—because Reels keep users distracted while Meta tests more ad formats. LinkedIn amplifies comments that lengthen dwell and spark secondary replies, rewarding nuance but also controversy. These biases operate regardless of creator merit.

Like heroes petitioning Olympus, you must craft offerings aligned with divine appetite. A brilliant essay posted on algorithm-hostile terrain will wither. A mediocre joke packaged in the platform's newest toy might flourish. Excellence matters, but placement matters first.

---

2 Dissecting Ranking Levers on Major Networks

We examine each network through three lenses: **Core Metric**, **Favored Form**, **Hidden Valve** (often-ignored tweak that jolts distribution).

2.1 YouTube

Core Metric: Average percentage viewed *per video* and *per session*.

Favored Form:

- 8–14-minute story-arc essays with pattern interrupts every 20-30 seconds.

- Playlist chains promoting serial binge.

Hidden Valve:

- "Key moments" chapters. When you add timestamp chapters, YouTube surfaces clips in search thumbnails. Making a curiosity-loaded chapter label ("Why Project Fails Here") spikes CTR without clickbait.

2.2 TikTok

Core Metric: Completion rate within first 5 seconds, re-watch loops, plus share-through to Dark Social (copies, DMs).

Favored Form:

- 7–40 second bursts, text-overlay telegraphing payoff.

- Content that demos or dramatizes trending audio within first beat.

Hidden Valve:

- Reply-via-duet. Publicly answering top comment with a duet amplifies the original's ranking as well as the new post's.

2.3 Instagram

Core Metric: Saves and send-privates.

Favored Form:

- Carousels that teach stepwise.

- Reels repurposed from TikTok but trimmed to remove competitor watermark.

Hidden Valve:

- Alt-text keywording. Adding descriptive alt text not only aids accessibility but quietly feeds Explore search.

2.4   X (formerly Twitter)

Core Metric: Retweets weighted by "Blue verified" accounts, then replies.

Favored Form:

- Long native posts ("Notes") stitched to ten-tweet hooks.

- Visual quote cards summarizing a thread.

Hidden Valve:

- Bookmark count. Elon's team has signaled bookmarks as private "intent" ranking. Prompting "bookmark this for Friday" can double distribution.

2.5   LinkedIn

Core Metric: Dwell time measured in milliseconds on feed.

Favored Form:

- Narrative posts 1,200–1,500 characters, broken by white-space lines.

- PDF carousels (a misnamed multi-slide doc) auto-played within feed.

Hidden Valve:

- Out-of-network shares. If someone with a different industry tag shares your post, LinkedIn tests it in new verticals at high weight.

2.6   Substack / Email

Core Metric: Open-to-click ratio across 6-week rolling window.

Favored Form:

- Consistent day-of-week drop.

- Cross-publication recommendations.

Hidden Valve:

- "Notes" micro-posts for warm leads. Substack's internal social timeline surfaces your letter to non-subscribers if engagement spikes within first 30 minutes.

2.7   Medium

Core Metric: Member reading time.

Favored Form:

- 5- to 7-minute reading-time essays with bold subheads.

- Intersection tags (e.g., "UX" + "Poetry").

Hidden Valve:

- Curation by in-house editors triggers email blasts. Include standout quote early; editors copy-paste for newsletters.

---

3   Reading Platform Weather: Spotting Favor Shifts

"Bright-eyed Athena turned her gaze,
 and suddenly the spears of Greeks found gaps in
 Trojan bronze."

Modern signs replace omens of birds and bowls:

1. **Feature Rollouts:** When a network unveils a format (Reels, Shorts, LinkedIn Articles), algorithm over-feeds it to seed adoption. Early adopters ride free impressions.

2. **Creator Insider Leaks:** YouTube's Creator Insider channel drops hints. TikTok staff tweet screenshot winks. Collect these.

3. **Patch Notes & Bug Fixes:** LinkedIn's engineering blog references ranking "improvements," often telegraphing metric shifts.

4. **Audience Behavior Anomalies:** Sudden spike in "likes but not clicks" may indicate feed rewarding quick emoji taps; pivot to CTA that warms scroll rather than link-out.

5. **Competitor Surge:** If a rival's similar content quadruples reach overnight, inspect their format. They may have latched onto a fresh lever.

Keep a log. Treat each pattern like shifting winds on the plain.

---

4   The Quarterly Divine Favor Audit

Every ninety days perform a structured ritual to map which platform gods smile or frown. Steps:

4.1   Gather Offerings (Data)

- Export analytics dashboards for each platform: impressions, reach, retention, reactions, shares, saves.

- Pull top-performing content pieces.

- Collect external announcements (feature launches, policy updates).

4.2 Read the Entrails (Analysis)

1. **Spike Matrix:** Which metrics rose >25 % despite similar effort? Note correlated formats.

2. **Fade Matrix:** Which formerly strong metrics dipped?

3. **Outlier Content:** Identify any post far above baseline—deconstruct length, topic, thumbnail.

4.3 Consult the Augurs (Peers)

Host a round-table with three fellow creators. Compare spikes and fades. Consensus reveals platform-wide changes versus personal variance.

4.4 Offer Sacrifice (Adaptation Plan)

For each platform, choose one new experiment aligned with favored lever. Example: YouTube retention fell yet Shorts watch-time soared—decide to serialize Shorts bridging to long video. Schedule tests.

4.5 Inscribe the Omens (Documentation)

Write a two-page brief summarizing findings, experiments, sunset formats. Archive in a "Favor Chronicle." Over a year, chronicles expose macro trends you otherwise feel only as chaos.

5   Case Study: Illustrator "Lyra" Surfs an Algorithmic Tide

Lyra posted time-lapse drawings on Instagram for years. Engagement plateaued. In Audit Q1 she noticed Saves on carousels outranked Likes on videos. She switched: converted each time-lapse into step-by-step storyboard carousel, overlaying mini-tips. Saves tripled; Explore impressions doubled. In Q2 Instagram launched Reels Bonus. Lyra carved 15-second process slices out of the same raw footage, added trending audio. Follower influx surged 40 %. By Q3, Reels matured and reach cooled, but her carousels held. Audit taught her to chase divine favor early and then maintain evergreen strongholds.

---

6   Ethics of Appeasing the Gods Without Losing Your Soul

Zeus can be fickle; creators risk contorting art into algorithm fodder. Balance with:

- **One-Third Rule:** Only one third of output optimized for current lever; one third evergreen craft; one third experimental play.

- **Mission Touchstone:** Re-read your macro vision (see Chapter 4) before adopting a trend. If the lever clashes with ethos, abstain.

- **Audience Respect:** Manipulative tactics (clickbait, rage-bait) burn long-term trust, and gods eventually pivot away from them. Remember Zeus struck oath-breakers with lightning.

---

7 Practical Toolkit – Building a "Weather Station"

7.1 Dashboards

Use no-code tools like Looker Studio to pull multi-platform KPIs into one view. Highlight anomalies in red/green.

7.2 RSS Scraper Feed

Track official engineering blogs, Creator Insider, TikTok newsrooms. Pipe into Slack.

7.3 Social Listening Column

Set TweetDeck search for "algorithm update" + platform name.

7.4 Peer Signal Chat

Create a small Discord where creators drop screenshot data points: "LinkedIn carousel reach x2 today?" Over time, these whispers cohere.

8 Exercises

1. **Bias Mapping** – Choose one platform. In 15 minutes write a blind hypothesis of its top three ranking levers. Pull analytics for last 60 days to confirm/refute.

2. **Mini-Audit** – Run a single-post A/B: one optimized to perceived bias, one ignoring. Measure delta in reach.

3. **Oracle Letter** – Draft a memo from "Future You 12 months ahead" describing which lever dominated and how you leveraged it. Reflect quarterly.

9 Pitfalls and Counter-Moves

- **Over-Pivoting:** dumping proven formats for every shiny feature. Counter: keep archival performance logs; sunset content only after three audits confirm stall.

- **Platform Dependency:** building all growth on one network's favor. Counter: diversify at least two channels; treat email list as sanctuary not ruled by gods.

- **Signal Noise:** misreading random spike as systemic change. Counter: require two data points and peer corroboration before strategic shift.

Closing Invocation

"So the fate of armies swayed on shining balances,
    and the wise who watched the scale adjusted stance,
    shields lifted where the heavier dish sank."

You cannot move Zeus's hand, but you can watch its tilt. Read the signs, audit the winds, and craft content trimmed to catch the climb. Do this every quarter, and while others blame mystery for their slump, you will already be marching under clear sky, bronze spears glinting in algorithmic sun.

Chapter 11 – Athena vs Ares: Content Formats for Strategy and Spectacle

> "Athena, whose mind knows all arts of war,
> and Ares, breaker of men, twin whirlwinds on the
> field."

In Homer's epic the two war-gods make a study in contrast. Athena plans, advises, and angles every strike so that a single spear-point topples an army. Ares charges in shouting, red-mist rising, thirsty for clamor and blood. The Greeks revere both energies. Without Ares nothing begins; without Athena nothing endures.

Your content ecosystem needs the same dual-engine. Strategic pieces—Athena's handiwork—are thought-through, evergreen, optimized for search and long-tail discovery. Spectacle posts—Ares in digital armor—erupt around trends, memes, live events, and algorithmic surges. Lean only on Athena and you risk invisibility, slow organic creep while others steal attention. Lean only on Ares and you spike, burn out, and vanish from feeds the moment noise shifts. Master the balance and your brand fights with wisdom and ferocity at once.

1 Mapping the Energies

1.1 Athena: Cunning, Calculated, Compound

She stalks the flank, whispers to Odysseus, times the counter-blow. In content terms:

- Evergreen guides that answer perennial pain.

- SEO-rich tutorials keyed to questions audiences ask monthly or yearly.

- Cornerstone essays that set thought leadership and earn backlinks.

- Long-form podcasts trimmed into searchable chapters.

- Case studies updated quarterly with fresh data.

These works compound; they receive cumulative traffic and authority and continue converting new visitors long after publish date.

> "Bright-eyed goddess held his hand and said: 'Wait. Strike when the shield glints just so.'"

1.2 Ares: Raw, Reactive, Flash

He roars from cloud to ground in one thunderous leap. Content equivalents:

- Live-tweet storms during conferences, playoff games, Apple keynotes.

- Meme riffs within hours of a viral video.

- Hot-take shorts reacting to breaking regulation or celebrity fiasco.

- Poll battles that pit two opinions and close before the cycle turns.

- Behind-the-scenes reels shot on a phone and posted the same afternoon.

These pieces spike impressions, juice follower counts, and create ambient buzz. They rarely rank in search after a week, but the immediate adrenaline keeps community pulse high.

> "Then Ares screamed, a bronze tornado,
> shaking all ranks merely by his presence."

---

2 Designing a Dual-Format Arsenal

2.1 Strategic Content Principles

1. **Topic Permanence** – Choose themes certain to remain relevant next year. Example: "How to price freelance design" outlasts "What the 2025 iPhone reveal means."

2. **Research Depth** – Cite studies, run original surveys, embed schema markup so search engines comprehend hierarchy.

3. **Update Cadence** – Schedule small revisions every quarter; keep the timestamp current. Athena polishes her spearhead, never lets it dull.

4. **Repurposability** – Build in modular chunks: intro, numbered sections, takeaway boxes. These convert easily into carousels or newsletter digests.

5. **Call-to-Action Ladder** – Because traffic drips over months, design CTAs for various awareness stages: lead magnet > webinar > premium offer.

2.2 Spectacle Content Principles

1. **Speed Over Polish** – Ninety percent timely beats one-hundred percent perfect posted tomorrow.

2. **Platform Native** – Match the hotspot: TikTok for dances, Threads for meme banter, YouTube Live for product teardown.

3. **Emotion Hook** – Aim for awe, laughter, outrage, or FOMO inside first three seconds. Ares swings for gut reaction.

4. **Conversation Catalyst** – Prompt comment battles, duet invites, Q&A stickers. Reaction fuels reach.

5. **Disposable CTA** – Push low-friction action suited to impulse ("vote," "tag a friend," "bookmark"). Deeper funnels come later via retargeting.

---

3 Crafting a Balanced Publishing Calendar

Homer's war rolls out in seasons—raids at dawn, councils by night. Your schedule must weave cunning and fury within each cycle. Below is a narrative template you can adapt. It outlines one quarter (twelve weeks) viewed as a campaign, then zooms to a standard week. Replace labels with your niche specifics.

3.1 Quarterly Arc

Week 1–2: Foundation Block
Publish one cornerstone article or flagship video—Athena's marble temple.
Simultaneously schedule three related micro-spectacles: a reaction reel teasing the guide, a poll asking followers where they struggle, a meme referencing the pain.

Week 3–4: Satellite Series
Break cornerstone into smaller SEO bloglets or carousel slides (Athena) while live-streaming a behind-the-scenes creation sprint (Ares). Clip highlight fails for TikTok.

Week 5–6: Mid-Campaign Surge

Introduce guest collaboration (Trojan Horse from Chapter 9) that expands reach; treat the launch day like a festival—live AMA, giveaway, trending hashtag.

Week 7–8: Data Harvest

Analyze engagement, pick one strategic piece showing traction; update stats, add interactive calculator. Reactively address any industry news through short posts linking back to that piece.

Week 9–10: Personal Story Arc

Publish a vulnerable essay or documentary vlog (Athena in storyteller garb) and pair it with two comedic skits (Ares) riffing on your own mishaps.

Week 11–12: Round-up and Forecast

Compile best Athena pieces into PDF lead magnet; host a live countdown of top spectacle moments—viewers vote for "Ares Clip of the Quarter." Finish with teaser trailer for next quarter's theme.

3.2   Weekly Rhythm Snap-Shot

Monday – **Strategic Pulse**
Morning: email newsletter summarizing one evergreen concept. Evening: schedule social teaser.

Tuesday – **Spectacle Burst**
A midday hot-take thread about fresh headline, with GIF and quote-tweet prompts.

Wednesday – **Hybrid Workshop**
Publish tutorial YouTube video; simultaneously run Instagram Live Q&A to hype it.

Thursday – **Micro-Strategic**
LinkedIn carousel built from Monday's newsletter but reframed for B2B audience.

Friday – **Spectacle Wrap**
Trend recap meme or duet. Poll: "Which clip should become next week's deep dive?" Builds user-generated roadmap.

Weekend – **Athena Maintenance**
Edit next month's SEO pillar, update alt text, outreach for backlinks—quiet temple work.

This pattern allocates roughly 60 percent Athena effort (deep pieces, maintenance, repurposing) and 40 percent Ares bursts (fast reactive posts). Adjust ratios by season; product launches might flip to 40/60 for short windows.

---

4   Workflow Integration and Team Roles

When armies combine horse and foot, coordination prevents friendly fire. Assign roles:

- **Strategic Lead** – researches, outlines, optimizes, schedules evergreen content.

- **Spectacle Scout** – monitors trends, crafts rapid responses, owns social quick-publish permissions.

- **Integration Producer** – slices strategic pillars into spectacle fragments, tags assets, manages calendar.

Even if you are a solo creator, wear these hats consciously, blocking separate hours: Monday mornings as Athena, Tuesday afternoons as Ares, Wednesday integration.

---

5 Metrics and Feedback Loops

Measure Athena outputs on:

- Organic search traffic.

- Backlinks and domain authority.

- Newsletter subscriber long-term open rate.

- Evergreen conversion to product.

Measure Ares on:

- 24-hour reach.

- Follower delta.

- Comment velocity.

- Share ratio (public and private).

Every Sunday compare these dashboards. Decide if spectacle surges justify pivoting next week's strategic topic (e.g., viral poll uncovers new keyword cluster).

---

6   Case Illustration: "CodeSage" Tech Educator

Athena assets – An ultimate guide to "Dependency Injection in Python" ranks page one for eighteen months; quarterly refresh pushes domain authority up.

Ares surges – When NASA's rover tweets Python snippets, CodeSage fires a 30-second TikTok explaining each line; clip hits two million views.

Balance – TikTok hype drives 12 k new eyes to the evergreen guide; 700 become course students over six weeks. Without Athena these eyeballs disperse; without Ares they never arrive.

---

7   Common Pitfalls

1. **Athena Over-Planning** – perfecting evergreen drafts for months; audience forgets you. Remedy: impose 45-day ceiling on pillars.

2. **Ares Burnout** – chasing every meme; message dilution. Remedy: cap reactive pieces at three per week; double-check if each ties back to mission.

3. **Format Clash** – posting 3,000-word essay on TikTok. Remedy: respect native dialects; convert long form to 60-second voiceover bullets.

4. **Calendar Creep** – backlog piles up. Remedy: quarterly "Divine Favor Audit" (Chapter 10) includes slot for timeline pruning.

8   Exercises

1. **Inventory Audit:** List last 20 posts. Mark S for Strategic, X for Spectacle. Aim for 60/40 mix next month.

2. **Format Swap Drill:** Take one Athena article; strip five micro-clips for Ares channels. Reverse: pick one viral meme you posted; write 1,000-word evergreen explainer.

3. **Calendar Draft:** In plain text, write a twelve-week plan assigning at least one pillar and three spectacles per week. Hang near desk.

Closing Invocation

"And where Athena's spear met Ares' shield
the clang was thunder in mortal ears,
but Greeks cheered, for wisdom and fury
marched together beneath their banners."

Do likewise. Let wisdom craft monuments that survive storms; let fury fire signal flares that summon the world to see them. In that harmony of planned marble and sudden lightning, your audience will find not just information but an ongoing saga—one they will fight to remain a part of, long after the latest trend scrolls out of sight.

Chapter 12 – Shields of Silver Light: Paid Boosts & Patronage

> "Then Thetis, the silver-footed, rose from the sea
> and set before Achilles the gleaming mail
> Homer calls 'shields of silver light,' fit for a god."

Achilles' new armor arrives by patronage—Hephaestus hammers bronze at a divine mother's request. Mortal hands could not forge gear so radiant, nor could Achilles win his ultimate duel without it. Homer folds a blunt truth into the poetry: even the mightiest talent sometimes needs outside resources. The gods gift the armor; Achilles still swings the spear. So with modern content: organic reach, craft, and grit remain the hero's muscle, yet selective injections of paid spend or patron support can plate that muscle in radiant scale.

This chapter trains you to wield paid amplification as a tool, not a crutch. We break the journey into three beats—**micro-budget testing → hero-budget scaling, retargeting campfires before broad conquest**, and **ethics that keep a creator mortal, sane, and trusted**. By the end you will run ads or court patrons without selling your voice, your mission, or your audience's goodwill.

1   The Lesson Revisited—Gods Gift Armor; Sometimes You Pay to Play

Athena slips Odysseus a thought, Poseidon lifts Greek ships on a wave, Hera blinds Zeus at a critical hour. Divine nudges are not equal to the hero's will, but they matter. Likewise, today's platforms tilt toward those who pay rent in the form of ad spend. They will swear otherwise in public statements. Ignore that politicking. Paid reach is the shimmer that catches a bigger sunbeam; organic craft then decides who stays looking. Investments can be micro—five dollars behind a carousel—or cosmic—six-figure brand deals. What matters is **intentionality**: buy specific momentum with clear expectation of learning or compounding return, never buy vanity impressions for ego heat.

> "Brightly it shone, and all the Greeks marveled;
> yet Achilles knew the shield's worth lay not in shine
> but in how it turned the point of the coming spear."

The shine is CPM. The point turned is revenue, list growth, or cause adoption.

---

2   Framework Overview

1. **Micro-Budget Testing** – drop coins sparingly, learn audiences, hooks, platforms.

2. **Hero-Budget Scaling** – once proof appears, pour targeted coin in pulses tied to product or campaign arcs.

3. **Retargeting Campfires** – warm those who already sat at your hearth before marching banners into cold lands.

4. **Ethic Guardrails** – keep spending subordinate to craft; keep disclosures clear; keep exit plan alive.

---

3 Phase One: Micro-Budget Testing

3.1 Define the Learning Hypothesis

Every five-dollar test must answer a question:
Which headline converts best for my webinar signup?
Does my audience skew Travel-TikTok or Finance-TikTok?
Will a 15-second vertical teaser outperform a 30-second story montage?

Write the hypothesis down, like a scout's map edge. Without it, you drown in vanity noise.

3.2 Choose the Controlled Variables

Keep **one variable** fluid. Freeze the rest: same creative on two audiences or two creatives at identical budget. Achilles wouldn't train footspeed and spear-thrust in the same drill; data muddies.

Budget Ratios

- Daily spend: 2 × target CPA at minimum.

- Duration: 72 hours to collect enough impressions unless niche micro-audience demands longer.

3.3 Execution

1. Load campaign on platform of choice.

2. Exclude existing followers if the test is purely for cold hooks; include them if you're comparing warm vs cold CTR.

3. Let run untouched—peeking and tweaking mid-flight resets learning algorithms.

3.4 Interpreting the Auguries

> "Hephaestus etched on the shield two cities,
> one at war, one at peace; Achilles would read omens
> in each gleam."

Metrics stand for omens:

- CPM reveals auction competition heat.

- CTR shows hook resonance.

- CPC hints cost of message per eyeball.

- Conversion Rate marks spear penetration.

Declare winner only if it beats the alternative by margin beyond noise—roughly 20 percent or 95 percent confidence.

---

4 Phase Two: Hero-Budget Scaling

You found a spear-point. Now temper it into a full phalanx.

4.1 Budget Escalation Ladder

Step	Spend Multiplier	Rule of Thumb
Seed	Base × 1	Proven micro ad ($5–15/day)
Sprint	× 3–5	After 3 days of stable results
Surge	× 10	Tie to product launch, 7-day pulse
Sustain	Variable	Drop to ROI-optimized level for tail

(Chart provided here narratively, not as a table in-render; visualize a rising ladder.)

4.2 Creative Flywheel

During each scaling step, refresh at least one creative unit so frequency doesn't breed blindness. Borrow from Chapter 11's Ares content to craft reactive variants—same CTA, new headline referencing current event. Keep Athena's evergreen piece untouched to anchor conversions.

4.3 Distribution Channels

- **Meta Ads** – broad demo, interest stack.

- **Google Search/P-Max** – capture bottom-funnel leads on evergreen queries.

- **YouTube TrueView** – high watch-time audiences for complex topics.

- **Newsletter Swaps / Paid Sponsorships** – rent trust from aligned curators.

Each channel is a shield segment; together they cover flanks.

---

5 Retargeting Campfires Before Broad Conquest

A campfire is anyone who engaged before: watched 50 percent of a video, visited your sales page, clicked newsletter but did not buy. They already feel your heat.

5.1   Segmenting Warm Circles

1. **Embers (hot):** Checkout abandoners, email clickers.

2. **Coals (warm):** 25 percent-plus video viewers, Instagram profile visitors.

3. **Smoke (lukewarm):** Three-second video viewers, scroll-thru social engagers.

5.2   Message Hierarchy

- **Embers** receive urgency: *"Your cart waits—seat claims close in 6 hours."*

- **Coals** receive proof: testimonial carousels, mini-case videos.

- **Smoke** receives value: free guide or webinar, no sale ask yet.

Set frequency caps—no mortal endures the same pre-roll five times a day without rage. Ten impressions per seven days is upper bound.

5.3   Campfire Lookalikes

After extracting juice from campfires, ask platforms for 3 – 5 percent similarity clones. This leaps beyond walls with a torch in hand.

6 Ethics: Stay Mortal—Don't Overdepend on Spend

"No man, though wrought with gold, may stand if pride draws him to strike the very gods that armed him."

6.1 Transparency

Mark sponsored posts; disclose affiliate links; label paid webinars clearly. Hidden motives rust reputation faster than algorithm declines.

6.2 Budget Discipline

Set a ceiling: **never exceed 30 percent of trailing-quarter revenue** on ads unless launch window recoups within 45 days. Achilles still owns spearcraft; the armor aids but costs no soul.

6.3 Creative over Cash

If ROI slips, address hook weakness or landing-page clarity before pumping more coins. Paid traffic magnifies flaws; fix craft, then reopen spend.

6.4 Patron Alignment

If courting patrons—sponsors, angel investors, grant foundations—run the "Mythos Fit" test (Chapter 1). Ask: would my north-star wrath line survive on their banner? If not, decline. Trojan gold weighs heavy when values conflict.

---

7 Case Study—"SyntaxSmith" Course Launch

Scenario: SyntaxSmith sells a $297 JavaScript mastery cohort. Organic wait-list: 1,200.

Micro-Tests:

- Headline A: "Stop Copy-Pasting StackOverflow." CTR 2.3 %.

- Headline B: "Write Code You're Proud Of." CTR 1.1 %.

A wins; CPC $0.88 on $10/day budget.

Hero-Scaling: $150/day for seven-day cart open. CPAs hold at $24; 310 seats sell; ad spend $1,050 returns $92k.

Campfire Retargeting:

- Embers (checkout abandon) saw 15-second "Your future self is waiting" clip; 41 % converted.

- Coals received carousel of alumni salary jumps.

- Smoke offered free "Debug Diary" PDF.

Ethics Steps: Labeled "sponsored" on Instagram stories; kept ad budget 12 % of projected revenue; used subscriber poll to choose next cohort module before relaunch.

Result: no list fatigue, high NPS, sponsor win—a code-editor company funded scholarships without dictating curriculum.

---

8 Guardrails Against the Siren Song

1. **Diminishing Return Watch:** If spend up 20 % but conversions flat, lower or pause. Platforms love plateaus.

2. **Quality Score Drift:** Google penalizes irrelevant ads; maintain landing message match.

3. **Audience Size Decay:** Reuse of lookalikes eventually yields lower intent; shake by new creative hooks or widen seed.

4. **Personal Brand Hollowing:** If organic posts drop from 3/week to 0 because ad ROI feels easy, momentum atrophies. Schedule consistent free value.

---

9 Tools and Rituals

- **Scripts:** UTM tracker cheat-sheet generator.

- **Dashboards:** Looker board pulling ROI per creative.

- **Alert Ritual:** Slack bot pings if CPA spikes 30 % above trailing seven-day average.

- **Audit Ceremony:** On the first workday each month, review spend vs revenue, creative fatigue, and ethical checklist.

---

10 Exercises

1. **Hypothesis Sheet:** Write three paid-test hypotheses; assign budget, metric, success thresholds.

2. **Ethics Pledge:** Draft a 200-word public statement on how you'll use paid reach; share with audience.

3. **Campfire Mapping:** Export last 180-day site traffic; tag by behavior; design three retarget ad copy lines for each heat tier.

4. **Hero Budget Blueprint:** If you had 10 × current spend, list exact allocations and timeline; notice where uncertainty creeps—research those gaps.

Closing Invocation

"And Achilles, brighter than noon sun in that new
armor,
 strode to battle, but still his mortal pulse beat under
bronze.
 So let your paid shields flash, yet let the hand that
wields them
 remember skin, sweat, and story are the true blade."

May your coins buy only what craft and conviction can wield. May
your patrons shape opportunity, not destiny. Wear silver light
proudly, but never forget the mortal heart inside the mail—its beat
is why audiences gathered in the first place, and why they will stay
when the last paid impression fades like gods withdrawing to
Olympus.

Chapter 13 – The Myrmidon Model: Building a Loyal Inner Circle

> "So the Myrmidons came on in their armour,
> a wedge of iron under the son of Peleus,
> each man sworn to follow where his captain led."

No company in the *Iliad* fights with tighter cohesion than Achilles' Myrmidons. They are not the largest force, nor do they hold royal titles, yet when Achilles finally unleashes them the plain shudders. Homer sketches their distinctive edge in three strokes: elite selection, personal devotion, and a shared identity forged by private ritual. Modern creators need the same strike team—an inner circle that receives your first drops, guards brand integrity, amplifies launches, and returns fire when trolls arrive. We will build that circle step-by-step, evolving casual readers into sworn comrades who proudly call themselves Myrmidons of your mission.

1   The Lesson: Achilles' Elite Unit

While Agamemnon labors to keep quarrelsome kings in line, Achilles speaks once and every Myrmidon rallies. He gives them bespoke armor, trains them apart from the rank and file, and honors their voices—Patroclus can question even the hero's rage. They, in turn, gift him something money cannot buy: unwavering advocacy.

"And they answered him with one shout that
splintered night—
  their captain's wrath was a home-fire in every chest."

Translate that loyalty into the creator economy:

- **Elite selection** → tiered memberships where belonging must be earned.

- **Personal devotion** → intimate channels (Discord lounges, premium letters) that reward candor.

- **Shared identity** → rituals, ranks, and game loops that turn contribution into social capital.

---

2 Crafting Membership Tiers

2.1 The Three-Ring Keep

- **Outer Ring – Followers**
  Free subscribers on the main platform. They witness the saga like townsfolk watching armies sail.

- **Middle Ring – Companions**
  Paid or application-based members who gain early drafts, behind-the-scenes, office-hours. Equivalent to Myrmidon foot-lancers.

- **Inner Keep – Lieutenants**
  A hand-picked cohort (1-5 % of audience) with direct
  strategic input, beta testing access, and revenue-share
  opportunities—Patroclus levels.

2.2   Designing the Gate Ritual

Belonging must feel won, not bought. Even if a tier carries a price,
layer an additional action:

1. **Vow Form** – ask each applicant to complete a short form:
   "What campaign of ours moved you most? Where can you
   aid the legion?"

2. **First Deed** – upon entry, new members perform a
   micro-quest: share a tip, review a resource, or post
   introduction video. Completion unlocks full channel
   visibility. This rite mirrors Myrmidon trainees proving worth
   in skirmish before real war.

2.3   Pricing Philosophy

Price not only for revenue but for *filtering friction*. If your brand
serves early-career designers you might charge $10/month for
Companion tier, $300/year for Lieutenant. If your niche is C-suite
AI ethics, $99/month and $2,500/year may attract the most serious
minds. Remember: smaller but sharper cohorts wield louder
spears.

3 Discord Circles: The Barracks of Bonding

Discord mimics the Greek camp better than email alone: tents (channels) for discussion, live voice firesides, roles for hierarchy.

3.1 Channel Architecture

- **#tactics-desk** – pinned resources; only you and lieutenants can post threads; others react with emojis.

- **#meal-mess** – casual chat, meme swaps.

- **#battle-report** – members log weekly wins; positive loop reinforces identity.

- **#whisper-council** – Lieutenants only; strategic talk, early access links.

3.2 Thread Rituals

At dawn every Monday, schedule a "Morning Muster" bot that prompts three check-in questions:

1. What spear are you sharpening this week?

2. Which foe (problem) worries you?

3. How can the legion lend shield?

Responses let you diagnose pain points for future content. Engagement metrics reveal potential lieutenants—those who help others before you do.

3.3 Voice Campaigns

Once a month fire up a 90-minute *Forge Night.* You walk members through a content build live—headline shaping, design tweaks—sharing screen while chat lobs feedback. Recording posted to #archives for late time-zones.

---

4 Premium Newsletters: The War Chronicle

> "And the heralds wrote the deeds on tablets,
> lest the flame of memory fade."

Your premium letter is the official chronicle of the Myrmidons. Objectives:

- Deliver knowledge not found in public feed.

- Preserve intimacy with direct voice—use "we," "our," address readers by first name tokens.

- Create a shareable teaser that allows lieutenants to lure worthy friends inside.

4.1 Template Anatomy

1. **Front Stanza – The Trumpet**
   100-word scene setter: quote, battlefield anecdote, startling stat.

2. **Field Orders – Tactical How-To**
   800-1,000 words deep-dive guide.

3. **Armor Polish – Resource Drop**
   One template, swipe, or discount code.

4. **Roll of Valor – Member Spotlight**
   Interview clip or screenshot of a companion's success story.

5. **Campfire Whisper – Upcoming Intel**
   One-sentence hint of next letter topic; hyperlink to suggestion board.

Publish cadence: bi-weekly. Too frequent dilutes; too sparse cools devotion.

4.2 Patron-Only Extras

Occasional *sealed scrolls*—audio memos or Loom demos—sent exclusively to Lieutenants. Limited distribution heightens status; they become your alt-press officers.

5 Gamifying Contribution

Gamification is not cartoonish XP bars; it is reputational circuitry that mirrors ancient honor culture.

5.1 Point Currency – "Obols"

Each act—answering a peer question, posting a resource, referring a friend—earns obols tracked by a simple bot. Publish leaderboard monthly. Top three receive physical token: enamel pin shaped like Myrmidon helm.

5.2 Badge System

Design five ascending titles:

1. **Scout** – joined, completed first deed.

2. **Spearman** – 50 obols, one peer testimonial.

3. **Shield-mate** – 150 obols, leads a study group.

4. **Veteran** – 300 obols, publishes guest essay in premium letter.

5. **Lieutenant** – invitation only, plus 500 obols or exceptional act.

Icons appear on Discord roles and next to name in newsletter shout-outs.

5.3   Seasonal Challenges

Quarterly *Bivouac Quests*:

- Draft three new carousels using our template and compare metrics.

- Pair up to host a co-working sprint.

- Build one local meetup of minimum five Myrmidons; share photo.

Rewards: digital badges, merch, or the chance to pitch a workshop under your brand banner—revenue split 60/40.

---

6   Elevating Lieutenants—From Followers to Co-Creators

"Patroclus, beloved brother-in-arms,
 you will wear my armor and command the men this day."

Lieutenants relieve you of tactical grunt work and extend capacity.

6.1   Selection Criteria

- Consistent high-value participation.

- Demonstrated alignment with brand voice.

- Ownership mindset: they propose solutions, not just seek them.

6.2   Responsibilities

1. **Moderation** – keep chat civil; defuse conflagrations.

2. **Beta Teams** – test new products, supply bug reports.

3. **Mentorship Pods** – each Lieutenant mentors 4–6 Companions; escalates standout talent to you.

4. **Public Representation** – guest on podcasts, speak at webinars, sign with "Lt." tag.

6.3   Compensation & Recognition

- Free top-tier membership.

- Profit share on any revenue their mentorship funnels.

- Annual "Shield-Forging Summit" retreat—cost covered, small group workshop.

- Personalized gifts: custom art, signed book preprints.

6.4 Succession Planning

If you step back for leave, a ranking Lieutenant acts interim host. This keeps rhythm unbroken, just as Patroclus wore Achilles' armor to sustain morale.

---

7 Operational Infrastructure

7.1 Tech Stack

- Discord (or Circle for all-in-one).

- Stripe + Memberful or Gumroad for tier billing.

- ConvertKit or Beehiiv for premium letter with built-in referral engine.

- Automations via Zapier: purchase→role assignment, obol logging, leaderboard updates.

7.2 Data Hygiene

Tag every member record with join date, tier, last engagement, obol count, referral count. Run monthly churn risk report: if a Companion's engagement drops 50 % two cycles, trigger "Shield Polish" email—personal nudge asking what support they need.

7.3 Security & Trust

Because inner circle materials may include unreleased IP, implement NDA clause in welcome pact. Keep channels encrypted; assign minimal admin rights. Publish code of honor; violations result in immediate revocation.

---

8 The Growth Flywheel

1. **Spectacle (Chapter 11) brings eyes.**

2. **Lead magnet funnels to outer ring.**

3. **Premium offer invites into Companion tier.**

4. **Gamification deepens retention.**

5. **Lieutenants broaden footprint—guest spots, collabs—starting loop again.**

Retention drives LTV, funds more content, and clarifies product decisions via feedback loops. Loss of one social algorithm update hurts little when 1,000 die-hard Myrmidons still rally each dawn.

---

9 Case Vignette: "WordSmith Guild"

Emma, a copywriting educator, created WordSmith Guild. Free list: 40k. Companion "Journeyman" tier: $20/month, includes Discord, template vault. Lieutenant "Master Artisan": invite only, 7 % of guild, helps grade monthly copy critiques. Within a year:

- Churn stabilized at 2 % monthly (industry average 8 %).

- 12 Guild-run regional meetups emerged, each with 30 + attendees.

- Journeymen revenue funded Emma's indie conference, which in turn attracted new readers, re-feeding the cycle.

The guild's voice now echoes Emma's language; memes, inside jokes, even brand colors propagate without her direct post. Achilles would nod.

---

10 Troubleshooting and Pitfalls

1. **Role Inflation** – too many badges lose meaning. Keep rarity sacred.

2. **Gate Snobs** – over-strict entry discourages new blood. Offer periodic open enrollment weeks.

3. **Lieutenant Burnout** – volunteers may tire. Rotate duties, schedule appreciation breaks.

4. **Echo Chamber** – inner circle bias blinds you to fresh perspectives. Host external critics quarterly.

---

11 Exercises to Start Building Today

1. **Draft Your Oath:** Write a 120-word vow new members recite or sign.

2. **Design Badge Names and Icons:** Sketch five titles; assign criteria.

3. **Map First 90 Days of Premium Newsletter Topics:** Ensure each letter triggers a community action.

4. **Identify Three Potential Lieutenants:** DM them with invitation to private call.

5. **Plan First Seasonal Challenge:** Choose objective, rules, timeline, reward.

Execute one exercise each week; by the next quarter, your campfires will crackle with new voices bearing your banner.

Closing Invocation

"And Achilles moved among them,
 not as a king above slaves, but as fire among
torches—
 one flame kindling a hundred until the night blazed
like noon."

Build your Myrmidons in that spirit. Kindle one torch, then another, until the brand's glow no longer needs your constant fuel. When storms come—as they always do—your inner circle will lock shields, steady the line, and carry your mission further than any lone hero could run.

Chapter 14 – Wrath to Reconciliation: Managing Burnout & Creative Rage

> "Rage—sing, goddess, the rage of Achilles,
> that sent countless souls to Hades and left their
> bodies
> a feast for dogs and birds."

Achilles' anger drives the whole *Iliad.* It also shatters him. He sulks alone while comrades die, he slaughters in a frenzy that leaves the Scamander river choked with corpses, and when the red haze clears, emptiness swallows the hero who could not modulate his own flame. Creators confront the same paradox. The fuel that powers obsessive craft can, unchecked, torch health, relationships, and the creative well itself. This chapter teaches you to transmute wrath into renewable heat—recognizing warning sparks, enforcing rhythms of rest, and engineering systems that protect both output and soul.

1 The Anatomy of Creative Rage

1.1 Source

Achilles' wrath erupts from two wounds: public insult by Agamemnon and private grief for Patroclus. In creators, rage often shoots from:

- **External invalidation** – algorithm kills a post, client slashes rates.

- **Internal breaches** – perfectionism detects flaw, imposter syndrome mocks success.

1.2 Symptoms

"And the heart in his chest was like live coals."

- Sleepless scroll through analytics.

- Sarcastic replies to harmless comments.

- Spiking output then collapse.

- Joyless completion of once-beloved tasks.

1.3 Consequences

Unchecked rage births burnout—physical exhaustion plus psychic numbness. Patroclus' death is Achilles' tipping point; your tipping point might be a missed launch, a failed sponsorship, or simply the day you wake loathing the dashboard that once glinted with possibility.

---

2   Practices for Prevention & Repair

2.1   Creative Sabbath

Definition: One full day per week without publishing, analytics, or ideation.

- *Philosophy:* In Homer, warriors pause to bury the dead. That interval renews courage.

- *Implementation:*

    - Remove platform apps from phone for 24 hours.

    - Engage hands—cook, garden, sculpt—because tactile acts soothe neural circuits fried by abstract metrics.

    - Journal without agenda.

"And they ceased from fighting and piled high the funeral pyre,
  pouring wine on the earth for the weary dead."

2.2   "Shield-Down" Weeks

Just as Achilles' shield glitters only when raised, your brand can dim without disappearing.

- *Frequency:* Every eighth week (roughly once a quarter).

- *Protocol:*

    1. **Announce:** Tell audience, "Recharge week—best hits will replay."

    2. **Replay Automations:** Schedule evergreen posts or curated archives.

    3. **Input-Only Mode:** Read books, attend workshops, wander museums.

    4. **Reflect:** On Friday, jot three insights gleaned; feed them into next sprint backlog.

2.3   Content Batching

Batching erects buffer zones so unexpected storms don't derail you.

- **Athena Day (Strategy):** Outline three weeks of topics.

- **Hephaestus Day (Production):** Record/ write multiple drafts.

- **Hermes Morning (Distribution):** Pre-load into schedulers.

Even if rage or illness strikes, the queue holds the line until you stabilize.

2.4 Rage Journaling Ritual

At any flash of fury, open a physical notebook—call it *Phthia Ledger* (Phthia: Achilles' homeland). Free-write the trigger, emotion texture, and an action you can control. Close book, do push-ups or breathing drill, return only when pulse slows. The page traps venom like Trojan sand swallowing blood.

---

3 Metrics: Establishing Red-Line Thresholds

> "The heart within him stormed,
> knowing he must choose quick death or lingering shame."

Data can either warn or whip. Define thresholds that signal time to step back before breakdown.

3.1   Engagement Red-Lines

Metric	Warning	Critical
Daily screen time	> 3 hr	> 5 hr
Comment response latency	< 5 min average	compulsive refresh
Content backlog	< 3 days	0 buffer

(Write these privately—no public table needed.)

3.2   Mental-Health Red-Lines

- Sleep < 6 hours three nights running.

- Two consecutive meals skipped for work.

- Zero physical movement in 48 hours.

- Recurring comment cynicism ("This platform is trash") more than twice in a day.

When any critical threshold hits, trigger an automatic stop: post a "Shield-Down" notice, reschedule meetings, inform accountability partner.

3.3 Accountability Mechanisms

- **Buddy Pact** – exchange red-line dashboards with peer; they ping when you slip.

- **Mood Tracker Bot** – simple 1-5 rating each check-in; down-trend for a week signals sabbath.

- **Public Boundary Statement** – pin a note describing your pause policy so audience respects gaps.

---

4 Reconciliation: Harnessing Rage Instead of Suppressing

Achilles eventually reconciles by facing Priam, allowing grief to wash away wrath. Creators can transmute anger into fuel.

4.1 Turning Offense into Op-Ed

Channel the frustration into a structured essay: *"What Platform X Got Wrong About Y."* Outline facts, solutions, call-to-arms. Publishing converts heat into communal value and positions you as thought leader—not ranter.

4.2 Product "Wrath Sprints"

Dedicate a 48-hour sprint to build a template, plugin, or crash-course that answers the pain that sparked rage. Release free or pay-what-you-want. The act reclaims agency.

4.3 Dialogue, Not Duel

Invite the party who triggered fury—a critic, competitor—into a live conversation (see Chapter 7). Curiosity often dissolves resentment, and audience gains nuanced discourse.

---

5 Case Study: "PixelFury" Designer

PixelFury's reel tanked after algorithm tweak; rage spiraled to 4 a.m. doomscroll. She noticed red-line: three nights < 6 hr sleep. Triggered Shield-Down week. Bot posted best-of reels, she hiked mountains, scribbled analog sketches. On return, wrote essay dissecting algorithm changes—viral on LinkedIn. Rage transmuted to accreditation; new clients cited essay as trust signal.

---

6 Cultivating Long-Term Resilience

6.1 Seasonal Retreats

Once every six months, disconnect completely for 5–7 days.
Announce, delegate to lieutenants. Read physical
classics—maybe even *The Iliad.*

6.2 Multi-Channel Identity

Don't tie worth to a single metric or platform. If one falters, others
hold morale. Diversification is psychological armor.

6.3 Gratitude Inventory

At end of each week, write three audience interactions that
sparked joy. Gratitude neurologically counters rage pathways.

---

7 Exercises

1. **Sabbath Scheduling:** Block next four Sundays; plan
   offline activities.

2. **Red-Line Dashboard:** Build simple spreadsheet with
   columns for metrics above; set conditional-format alerts.

3. **Wrath Ledger Start:** Buy notebook, write first entry
   describing a recent irritation.

4. **Batch Blueprint:** In two hours, map next month's topic list
   and assign production dates.

Closing Invocation

> "And the anger in his chest ebbed like tide,
> grief entered, then calm; dawn found him
> resolved to fight clear-eyed, not blind."

May your own dawn find you the same. Keep wrath as spark, not
wildfire. Rest shields when bronze hums too hot, set watchful
metrics along the wall, and reconcile often—with self, with peers,
with purpose. In that balance lies creative longevity fiercer than
any single surge, and songs the Muse will still deem worth singing
when today's platforms crumble like fallen Troy.

Chapter 15 – Funeral Games for Patroclus: Turning Endings into Fresh Starts

"Then the son of Peleus rose in the midst and spoke:
  'Now, all you Argive captains, put by your sorrow;
  we honor Patroclus with contests of strength and speed,
  that his shade may rejoice and we who live may find new fire.'"

No one closes a narrative like Homer. When Patroclus falls, the poem halts its violence to hold an improvised Olympics on the sand. Chariot races thunder, wrestlers grapple, archers loose shafts, mugs of honey-sweet wine change hands. Grief does not vanish; it alchemizes into communal play. By the time the last garland settles on the victor's brow, the Achaeans stand taller. The war story resets its emotional baseline and rolls toward the climactic duel that ends the epic.

Too many modern creators treat an ending as a fade-out: project shipped, campaign done, silence until inspiration strikes again. The audience drifts, the momentum chills, and when the next launch finally surfaces it must rebuild trust from half-memory. Funeral Games offer a better pattern. They spin closure into renewal, turn post-project fatigue into spectacle, and seed the soil for whatever saga follows. This chapter will teach you to stage your own games—launch retrospectives that share honest metrics, season-finale giveaways that reward loyalty, and audience challenges that pull followers onto the field beside you. Finally, we'll lay planks for the exit ramp into your next arc so the crowd crosses over instead of peeling away.

---

1   The Lesson: Celebration as Continuity

Achilles orders games not to distract but to *complete* the chapter. War paused, grief named, achievement displayed: the arc lands. Creators can emulate three functions of Homer's scene:

1. **Commemoration** – Acknowledge the toil that built the finished work. Followers see you bleed; they deserve witness to the closing rites.

2. **Redistribution of Glory** – Achilles gifts golden mixing bowls, tripods, stallions. You will hand out prizes—knowledge, swag, shout-outs—so effort cycles back into the community.

3. **Reset of Tone** – Battles drain; games re-energize. After a heavy research series, a playful quiz cleanses palate; after an uproarious meme sprint, a reflective recap restores depth.

> "So spoke Achilles, and the crowd pressed close,
> eager for contest though shadows of grief still lay
> long."

Your fans likewise hunger for an outlet when a story ends. Offer them one, and they deliver their own content—testimonials, duets, reaction threads—that becomes the first spark of whatever's next.

---

2   Techniques for Modern Funeral Games

2.1   Launch Retrospectives

A retrospective is the chariot race of today's digital arena: velocity measured, hazards narrated, winners named. Yet most creators hide revenue, engagement, and failure behind generic thank-you posts. Transparency electrifies.

Anatomy of a Compelling Retro

- **Opening Hook** – Quote, screenshot, or metric that encapsulates the journey: "$127,893 in seven days… with one near-fatal bug."

- **Chronology Beat-Map** – Bullet timeline of pivotal moments: pre-launch panic, day-three plateau, influencer shout-out, midnight hotfix.

- **Number Scroll** – Break down: visitors, conversion, refund, ad spend, profit, community growth. Bold the unexpected (refunds might be lower than peers, or ads higher).

- **Behind-the-Curtain Photo** – Show the "shields stacked at dawn": your Trello board mid-chaos or the pizza boxes.

- **Lessons Cut Sharp** – No generic "work hard." State counterintuitive insight: "Discounting *after* wait-list signup doubled upsell."

- **Fan Acknowledgment Roll** – Screenshot tweets, Discord encouragements, bug reporters. Tag them.

- **Invitation** – "If you plan a similar launch, steal my sheet; link below."

Post the retro as: long-form blog, LinkedIn article, Twitter/X thread, or narrated YouTube slide deck. Encourage Q&A; answer publicly to extend life. The retro cements credibility and transforms private data into communal scholarship—Homer naming each driver as they enter the course.

2.2 "Season Finale" Giveaways

In Book 23 Achilles offers prizes tiered by feat. Your finale giveaway should likewise stratify to tap diverse follower appetites.

Design Principles

- **Thematic Relevance** – If your arc was about storytelling, prizes are Moleskine bundles, book consult calls, or license to a storyboarding tool.

- **Tier Diversity** – One grand prize (high-touch consult), three mid-prizes (swag boxes), many micro-prizes (template packs, digital stickers).

- **Skill and Chance Blend** – Ask entrants to perform a mini-task—share their favorite takeaway, remix a meme, write haiku—then random-draw winners within top manifold. This balances Achaean skill contests with the dice toss of Tyche.

- **Friction Calibration** – Lower friction for smaller prizes, higher for grand. Don't doom entry count with five-step funnels.

- **Visibility Window** – 72-hour entry, 24-hour winner announcement; urgency prevents fatigue.

Execution Steps

1. **Launch Post** – Carousel or video summarizing arc, announcing prizes, explaining entry.

2. **Midway Live Check-In** – Show entries in progress, address questions, stoke FOMO.

3. **Winner Stream** – Livestream wheel spin or bracket final; capture clips for socials.

4. **Fulfillment Thread** – Photo of packing boxes, shipping labels, digital code emails. Transparency reinforces trust.

Giveaways close the arc on a confetti note and flush algorithmic reach as entrants tag friends.

2.3   Audience Challenges

The funeral games are interactive content—they make spectators performers. Modern challenges convert audience from lurkers to co-creators.

Types of Challenges

- **Build-With-Me Sprint** – Participants replicate part of your project using your template or tutorial. Showcase before/after gallery.

- **Idea Tournament** – Crowds vote on feature proposals; top two advance to a debate you moderate (Chapter 7 tactics).

- **Scavenger Hunt** – Hide clues across old posts, encouraging re-reads; final code unlocks exclusive resource.

- **Creative Remix** – Provide asset pack (photos, lines of code, beats) and challenge audience to remix; public gallery becomes UGC trove.

Framing and Ritual

Announce challenge as an *honor to Patroclus*—not in name, but in ethos: completing the journey by demonstrating mastery. Offer badges or roles (Scout, Runner, Charioteer) and schedule closing ceremony where you screen-share hot entries, applaud, gift digital laurel wreath PNGs.

> "And the crowd roared when Eumelus' horses burst ahead,
> dust streaming, reins taut like fates."

Your community will roar in emoji when user "MaiDesigns" posts a stunning carousel birthed from your template.

---

3   Mapping the Exit Ramp to the Next Arc

Ending is seed. Homer uses games to pivot Achilles from wrath to purpose; next morning he goes to fight Hector. Your exit ramp must carry energy into the forthcoming campaign.

3.1   Teaser Breadcrumbs

Within the retro or giveaway finale, drop hints:

- "Notice how metric X spiked when we tried Y? We'll explore that in depth next month."

- Use blurred-out screenshots of sketches labelled *Phase 2*; invite guesses.

- Plant a poll: "Which realm do you want us to raid next—email automation or AI prompts?" Poll results pre-validate content path.

3.2   Inter-Arc Silence Management

Some stories need off-season rest. Communicate timeline: "Forge is cooling for two weeks; we return on August 1 with Campaign *Star-Flare*." Schedule mini-content—quotes, archived nuggets—to keep feed heartbeat faint but alive.

3.3   Beta Gate for Super-Fans

Offer early access to the next thing exclusively to challenge participants or giveaway entrants. They become vanguard, echoing Patroclus' role as first into battle wearing Achilles' armor. Their excitement spider-webs through the network, priming rest of audience.

3.4   Asset Recycling**

Collect datasets, lessons, and user creations from the games. These inform landing pages, nurture sequences, and PR pitches for the next launch. Nothing is wasted—ashes of Patroclus' pyre fertilize new grass.

---

4 Case Study: "InkForge" Season One → Season Two

InkForge, a writing-tool startup, spent twelve weeks releasing a chapter-a-week interactive fiction series to demonstrate software. Finale week:

1. **Retro Thread** shared read-through stats (2.1 million words read), bug logs, and top user quotes.

2. **Giveaway** offered engraved fountain pens and lifetime pro accounts. Entry task: submit a 150-word alternate ending. 4,700 entries.

3. **Audience Challenge** turned the best 30 endings into a public vote; grand winner's version became canon in an Easter-egg branch.

4. **Exit Tease**: retro concluded with blurred screenshot of upcoming "Visual Novel Mode," date T-30.

Result: 28 percent of finale participants joined wait-list for Season Two on day one.

5 Restorative and Strategic Benefits

- **Community Bonding** – participants watch each other compete, forging lateral ties.

- **Content Multiplication** – retros, clips, UGC add 20–40 fresh assets.

- **Algorithm Bump** – spikes at arc end mitigate plateau after heavy posting weeks.

- **Personal Closure** – creators celebrate instead of crashing into anticlimax, reducing chapter fatigue (see Chapter 14 burnout).

---

6 Potential Pitfalls and Safeguards

- **Prize Logistics Chaos** – plan shipping budget, tax implications. Keep digital as fallback.

- **Overlong Challenge** – momentum fizzles; keep under 14 days.

- **Retrospective Backfire** – transparency too raw (e.g., low revenue) can deter prospects. Counterbalance with lessons and roadmap improvements.

- **Teaser Over-Hype** – promise only what build timeline
  supports; delayed arcs erode trust.

---

7   Exercises

1. **Select End-of-Arc Date** for current project; mark calendar.

2. **Draft Retro Outline** with five metrics, three stories, and
    one surprising failure.

3. **Brainstorm Giveaway**: list three tiered prizes; tag each
    with logistics cost.

4. **Sketch Audience Challenge** concept in one paragraph.

5. **Write Teaser Line** foreshadowing next arc; test on trusted
    peer.

Complete within 48 hours; begin asset prep simultaneously with
project's final sprint so event feels organic, not bolted on.

Closing Invocation

"And as the fire died, new embers glowed;
   songs rose over cups, horses stamped for the road

ahead,
 and dawn's first gold kissed helms ready for the next
campaign."

Endings are embers, not ashes. Host your funeral games with pageantry and candor. Let metrics be medals, let followers race in friendly dust, let laughter heal the strains of the march. When the last wreath is lifted, show the horizon—and stride. Your narrative will roll uninterrupted, each finish line the starting gun for the story not yet told, just as Homer's games kindle the mood for Hector's final stand and the fall of Troy beyond. The Muse awaits your next verse; sing it with the crowd still cheering from the stands you built today.

Conclusion – The Song Lives On

"And he whose fame the Muses loved
never wholly dies, for every generation
finds his voice waiting in the wind."

Achilles is long dust, Troy a scatter of broken ramparts, yet the *Iliad* still sings. It sings because Homer shaped raw war scraps into pattern, rhythm, and meaning. He handed future storytellers a spine of human motives—honor, rage, grief, hope—and let them graft their own flesh on that frame. You have followed this book's fifteen chapters to discover how an ancient war chronicle can train a digital creator. Before we part, let the scroll unfurl one last time. We will gather the war's bright lessons, hand you the standard, and point toward the next campaign where *your* epic waits to be sung.

I. What the War Taught Us—A Quick March Past the Pillars

- **Summon the Muse.** Open with a north-star theme so clean the Muse can perch on it. Your *wrath line* is not anger alone; it is concentrated purpose.

- **Know Thy Achilles.** Dominate a niche by mapping your strongest gift onto a market gap. Sharpen that edge with sprints, protect it from hubris.

- **Honor & Hubris.** Build Troop Feedback Loops, gratitude threads, and crisis plans so pride powers you without poisoning the camp.

- **Hephaestus' Shield.** Forge brand depth in concentric rings: cosmic mission, recurring series, lexicon, and a visual grammar consistent as noon sun.

- **Epic Similes.** Frame ideas in metaphors that bite like lion fangs; write hooks that loop audience brains on replay.

- **Catalogue of Ships.** Transform lists into momentum using rhythm, pattern breaks, and serial formats that beat like war drums.

- **Duel Scenes.** Stage one-on-one debates, AMAs, and stitchable clips so whole armies halt to watch your spotlight anchor.

- **Rally the Achaeans.** Structure weekly content arcs—tension, consequence, renewal—so morale never sags and curiosity never sleeps.

- **Trojan Horse Tactics.** Slip partnership value inside gifts audiences hoist willingly; court overlap under thirty percent; nurture new allies through campfire funnels.

- **Olympian Politics.** Audit platform biases quarterly and surf algorithm winds like Odysseus reading gull wings.

- **Athena vs. Ares.** Balance evergreen strategy with spectacle bursts. Wisdom plans; fury demands attention.

The calendar is their treaty.

- **Shields of Silver Light.** Spend coins with intent—micro-tests, hero surges, campfire retargeting—while staying mortal and transparent.

- **The Myrmidon Model.** Grow an inner circle through tiers, Discord barracks, gamified roles, and lieutenant elevation, so loyalty outlives feed quirks.

- **Wrath to Reconciliation.** Enforce sabbaths, shield-down weeks, red-line metrics. Rage is spark, not wildfire.

- **Funeral Games.** Close arcs with contests, retros, giveaways, and challenges that spin endings into prologues.

If you remember nothing else, remember this: **story is system**. Homer's order—invocation, catalogue, duel, exhortation, feasting, funeral games—mirrors the rhythms that still glue eyeballs to screens. You have translated each pulse into a modern workflow.

II. The Open Gate—Crafting a Modern Epic in Your Own Niche

The hour has come to lift your own standard. You will find no Trojan prince to duel, but you will face algorithm tides, time thieves, self-doubt gatekeepers, and the siren song of comfort. Face them spear-forward. Here is your battle plan:

1. **Draft Your Invocation Today.** Spend twenty minutes chiseling a one-sentence theme. Print it, post it, or tattoo it on the inside of your laptop if you must.

2. **Select One Battlefield.** Choose the platform where your gift and your audience intersect best. Start there; expand only once the ground is yours.

3. **Forge Your Shield This Week.** Design brand visuals, lexicon, and a recurring series. Consistency builds temples faster than scattered marble blocks.

4. **Write One Epic Simile for Your Next Post.** If it sticks in your memory tomorrow morning, it will stick in theirs.

5. **Plan a Three-Episode Arc.** Map tension, consequence, renewal; schedule over the coming seven days.

6. **Identify a Trojan Horse Partner Within Thirty Days.** Draft the value gift; outline nurture path.

7. **Block Your First Sabbath.** Protect it whether numbers spike or slump.

8. **Set Red-Line Metrics and Share Them With a Peer.** The watchdog bark saves more than it interrupts.

9. **Sketch a Finale Giveaway for the Project After Next.** Know your end before you begin; endings shape effort and memory.

10. **Schedule Your First Divine Favor Audit Ninety Days Out.** Patterns trump hunches. Let data carve your prophecy.

Do these, and you stride from student to bard, from follower to warrior-poet.

III. Marching Orders—Tools and Communities That Await You

The book is parchment; life prefers stone and sweat. To embed these tactics in muscle we have prepared three ongoing supports.

1. The *Lessons from The Iliad* Workbook

- **What It Is:** A 120-page PDF/Notion hybrid stocked with fill-in worksheets, checklists, ritual prompts, and mini-case libraries.

- **Core Sections:**

    - Muse Invocation template with space for fifteen wrath-line drafts.

    - Achilles Edge matrix for gap identification.

    - Feedback Loop calendar automations.

- Shield mood-board snapshot pages.

- Epic Simile generator exercises.

- Arc storyboard grids.

- Divine Favor Audit dashboards pre-coded for Google Looker.

- **How to Get It:** Download link at the URL printed at the back of this book. Use access code *PATROCLUS* to unlock bonuses.

2. The Digital Phalanx Community

- **Platform:** Private Discord (or Circle if you choose softer UI).

- **Roles:** Wanderers (free), Companions (workbook purchasers), Myrmidons (annual pass), Lieutenants (hand-picked).

- **Channels:** #morning-mustering, #forge-nights, #funeral-games-planning, #divine-favor-alerts.

- **Live Events:**

  - Quarterly Trojan Horse Matchmaking mixer.

  - Monthly Duel Scenes featuring opposing experts.

- Weekly Ares Burst challenge—create a reaction reel in under two hours.

- **Purpose:** Practice, feedback, morale. This is the place to beta-test shield motifs or debrief after burnout glimmers.

3. Ongoing Mentorship Cohort

- **Structure:** Rolling 12-week sprints limited to twenty creators per cohort.

- **Phases:**

    - *Weeks 1–4*: Athena strategic build—north-star line, shield, evergreen pillar.

    - *Weeks 5–8*: Ares spectacle mastery—rapid video, live debate, meme science.

    - *Weeks 9–12*: Funeral-Game finale—launch, retro, giveaway, next-arc plan.

- **Deliverables:** Every member publishes a micro-epic by graduation: one complete campaign with documented metrics and community engagement.

- **Mentors:** Rotating panel of channel-specific veterans—YouTube strategist, newsletter savant, performance coach.

- **Admission:** Application plus "first deed" mini-challenge (write an epic simile tweet and achieve 1,000 impressions).

IV. Final Blessing—The Legacy You Now Steward

> "No one can hasten his fate, but each may earn a song."

The digital stage resets faster than any Bronze Age dawn. Tweets blow away like chaff, algorithms rewrite scroll order, servers change rulers. Yet story outlives its scaffolds. Homer's words crossed millennia carved on brittle papyrus, copied by monks, printed by Gutenberg, piped into school e-books. Your niche—be it data viz, street fashion, micro-farm permaculture, AI choreography—deserves an epic that distant readers can still use when today's icons vanish.

Write with that horizon. Compose for someone yet unborn who will find your backlog and, in some new language or sensory interface, hear your voice tell them, *"I too grappled with the gods of time and distraction, and here is how I carved a clearing."*

Carry the wrath line as compass, the shield as banner, the inner circle as family, the funeral games as festival, and the audits as oracle. You have armor, tactics, models, and maps. All that remains is the journey—and the journey begins the moment you close this book and speak your first line into the open air.

May the Muse hear it. May the gods grant a fair wind. May strangers at distant fires repeat it until your song, like Achilles', lives on, luminous in the ever-turning world.

THIS IS NOT A COLLECTION

This volume is part of **Ancient Wisdom Hacks**—
an ongoing body of work focused on how strategy, power, and
failure actually function under pressure.

The books are only one layer.

What you are reading is an entry point into a larger system of
interpretation, application, and expansion.

WHAT THESE WORKS ARE DESIGNED TO DO

Most people look for answers.

These works expose patterns:

- How decisions are made before they are visible
- How systems weaken before they collapse
- How power shifts before it is recognized

This is not theory.
It is applied observation.

THE SYSTEM BEHIND THE WORK

Across all volumes and future releases, three forces remain
constant:

- **Strategy** — how outcomes are shaped before action
- **Conflict** — how people and systems break under pressure
- **Power** — how control is gained, maintained, and lost

No single book contains the full picture.
Each adds another angle.

CONTINUE BEYOND THIS VOLUME

New interpretations, applied volumes, and extended works are released continuously.

To access current and future material, visit:

www.AncientWisdomHacks.com

WHAT YOU WILL FIND

- Additional applied volumes across industries
- Expanded interpretations of foundational texts
- New releases not available through standard distribution
- Future projects extending beyond books

The system is still expanding.

FINAL POSITION

Clarity does not make outcomes easier.

It removes the illusion that they were ever simple.

Ancient Wisdom Hacks
Interpretation over repetition.
Application over theory.